SURREGIONAL

EXPLORATIONS

W9-COB-827

MAX CAFARD

STEPHEN DUPLANTIER,
ILLUSTRATIONS & DESIGN

CHARLES H. KERR
PUBLISHING COMPANY
Established 1886. Chicago, Illinois

Copyright © 2012 by Max Cafard

ALL RIGHTS RESERVED. This book contains material protected under International and Federal Copyright Laws and Treaties. Any unauthorized reprint or use of this material is prohibited. No part of this book may be reproduced or transmitted in any form or by any means, electronic or mechanical, including photocopying, recording, or by any information storage and retrieval system without express written permission from the author and publisher.

Surregional Explorations
180 pp + vi
ISBN 978-0-88286-363-4

1. Philosophy. 2. Cultural Studies. 4. Political Science.
4. Surregionalism. 5. Surrealism. 6. Film Criticism.

Max Cafard, Author
Stephen Duplantier, Illustrations and Book Designer

Manufactured in the United States of America.

9 8 7 6 5 4 3 2 1

Citations from books and periodicals have been fairly used for scholarly and educational purposes. Some images have been used for purposes of parody, satire, and education.

Cover: Photo by Alexey Sergeev.
Campo Santo, St. Roch Cemetery, New Orleans.

Charles H. Kerr, Publishers
1726 West Jarvis Avenue.
Chicago, Illinois 60626
www.charleskerr.com
Subversive Literature for the Whole Family since 1886

CONTENTS

TO ERIS
GODDESS OF THE DIALECTIC,
REBELLION & CREATIVE
NEGATION.

PERSONIFICATION OF CHAOS
& DISORDER.

ESTRANGED SISTER OF
HARMONY.

Foreword

Philosopher, activist, artist *Max Cafard, has been steadily working his way through critiques of Anarchism, Surrealism, Situationism, Media, Cinema, and Regionalism, to arrive to his own fascinating and practicable practice of the Surregional. The still-standing techniques of all the -isms Cafard has not incinerated in his investigations have been patched to construct a mobile Surregional vehicle that is ecologically sound, civically festive, carnivalistically joyous, and socially just. It helps Surregionality that it takes for its area of action the city of New Orleans and the surrounding delta of the Mississippi River, a region with a fertile imaginary and abundant life (re)sources. Whether Surregional ideas work on an arrid terrain with historically rooted tribal conflicts supplied with modern weapons, is a debatable question, and worth debating. The exciting possibilities of speculation and action that the Cafard proposals open are very much here for the taking, playing with, mulling over, and using as projectiles or caresses. Surregionalism may even be the only way to stay human in the belly of the monster machine.*

ANDREI CODRESCU

Andrei Codrescu is the author of *The Posthuman Dada Guide: Tzara and Lenin Play Chess,* and many other books.

SURREGIONAL
EXPLORATIONS

Wú

Hell, 1952 by Robert Doisneau. Détournement by Stephen Duplantier

Deep Play in the City

CRITIQUE OF THE *DÉRIVE*
THE SITUATIONIST DRIFT, ADRIFT

Guy Debord describes the *dérive*, or *drift*, the classic Situationist mode of exploring the city, as "a *technique* of rapid passage through varied ambiances" involving "playful-constructive behavior and awareness of psychogeographical effects."[1] The *dérive* was central to Situationist urbanism and was part of a project of challenging the ways in which Spectacular-Commodity Society dominates our experience and our sensibilities, and envisioning a new city beyond the limits of the Spectacle. This project can only be seen as entirely admirable.

However, some questions arise about the adequacy of the *dérive* as a mode of experiencing the city, and as a means of pursuing this admirable project. Does the Situationist *dérive* maintain too much of a distance from the urban phenomena it encounters or might encounter? Does it lack a sufficient level of passionate attraction to the urban milieu? Is it too focused on the world of visible things to the neglect of other modes of experience? Does it sometimes lapse into an anti-spectacular spectacularism? Does it uncritically preserve a traditional one-sided, masculinist perspective, exalting its own world of "power and adventure"? Does it sometimes fail to escape that curse of late modernity, cynical rationality? Do you somehow already know what the answer to these all these questions is going to be?

1. All citations from Debord can be found in his "Théorie de la dérive" (December, 1958), trans. by Ken Knabb, online at http://www.bopsecrets.org/SI/2.derive.htm, with the exception of several that are taken from his "Report on the Construction of Situations and on the International Situationist Tendency's Conditions of Organization and Action"(June, 1957), trans. by Ken Knabb, online at http://www.bopsecrets.org/SI/report.htm.

Let us consider the idea of the *dérive* as: 1. "a technique"; 2. "of rapid passage"; and 3. "through varied ambiances." Some descriptions indicate that these qualities describe precisely the manner in which the Situationists carried out the *dérive*, either rushing around on foot or even taking taxis. But one must wonder why one would be in such a hurry if the point is to experience the city? Perhaps we should take inspiration from the "Slow Food Movement" and initiate a "Slow Foot Movement." Much of the appeal of the *dérive* is, after all, its driftlike quality, and *dérive rapide*, much like *cuisine rapide*, seems like a *contradictio in adjecto*.

Also, why must a *dérive* move not only with rapidity, but through "ambiences" in particular? This sounds rather suspiciously like sightseeing; and do we really need another *technique*, especially an italicized one? Perhaps we can't dispense entirely with means, but if the *dérive* were to slow down and become more patient and less goal directed, the *dériveur* might find more of what the city has to offer. [2]

The *dérive* can mean drifting outside the constraints of conventional perception. However, it can also mean going adrift and falling into the abyss at the far reaches of modernity. The *dérive* has sometimes drifted in the direction of proto-post-mortemism.[3] If we choose to go on a *dérive*, we must beware that it doesn't become a death *dérive*.

One sense of *dériver* is "to divert." But from what does the *dérive* divert us? The Situationist might reply that it diverts us, our experience and our lives, from the dominance of the Spectacle. This is the *dérive* as *détournment*. It's a detour well worth taking. But there is a moment of the *dérive*, a central, determining moment, in which it is diversion from the road we need to take, a detour from the way to the things themselves.

Perhaps the most obvious linguistic connection of *dériver* is with *la rive*. This term signifies a shore or bank, so *dériver* might suggest drifting away from the shore. And we do need to drift from the shore in order explore the many regions around us. However, we must at the same time remain *riverains*, inhabitants of our little place on the shore, for if we don't learn to have deep and intense experience of that place, will we be capable of doing so anywhere else?

It must be recognized that the *dérive* is also described as "technique

---

2. Generally, the term "dériveur" refers a dinghy, but it can also used to describe one who goes on a *dérive*. Very occasionally, as in the song "Dériveur" by the Belgian band Rose Cafard (www.cafardrose.be), it can refer to both.

3. On post-mortemism, see, for example, "Nietzschean Anarchism & the Post-Mortem Condition" in *The Surre(gion)alist Manifesto and Other Writings*, pp. 59-91.

of locomotion without a goal," a very promising idea—a means that is not a means toward anything in particular. Also quite admirably, we find that the *dérive* includes "playful-constructive behavior," so that it has something in common with a well-designed, or better, an undesigned or minimally designed children's playground (see the anarcho-urbanist idea of the Adventure Playground[4]). Best of all, it involves "awareness of psychogeographical effects," and thus it shares qualities of surregional exploration, in that it ushers one into the realm in which psychoregions and georegions intersect. And how is this geopsychic awareness attained? The participants, we are told, "let themselves be drawn by the attractions of the terrain and the encounters they find there." So at this point passion takes precedence over action, the emphasis is on being drawn and being acted upon, allowing oneself to be affected by the spirit of place, the power of things, the lure of the phenomena.

But Debord immediately falls into a pseudo-dialectical trap. He concludes that "the *dérive* includes both this letting-go and its necessary contradiction: the domination of psychogeographical variations by the knowledge and calculation of their possibilities." Some dialectics lead to neat syntheses, others lead to a balance or oscillation between opposing poles, but others lead to the utter annihilation of one or both of the contradictory terms. Some contradictions are in fact antagonistic and this unfortunately happens to be one of them. The quest for domination, including domination by means of supposed *savoir-faire* and calculative rationality, cannot coexist with a "letting-go," a passionate attraction that discovers an enchanted reality beyond itself, but instead annihilates the latter. Debord thinks that some sort of "ecological science, despite the narrow social space to which it limits itself, provides psycho-geography with abundant data." However, whatever ecological science he has in mind, far from providing any knowledge as domination of the phenomena, can give no more than hints of the infinitude of possibilities, and must coexist with the spirit of playful exploration, the spirit of the gift, and the cultivation of negative capability.

Henri Lefebvre, a major influence on and sometime collaborator with the Situationists, described in an interview his experience of the *dérive*. According to his account, in the *dérive* "one goes along in any direction and recounts what one sees." The goal, which he notes, "didn't

---

4. Classically described by anarchist urbanist Colin Ward in "A Parable of Anarchy: Adventure Playground," in *Anarchy* 7 (Sept.1961):193-201. Descriptions of existing adventure playgrounds can be found easily on the Internet.

always work," was "to attain a certain simultaneity" that would result in "a synchronic history." This cumulative history based on their collective experience is what the Situationists were aiming at in their idea of a "unitary urbanism." They would "unify what has a certain unity, but a lost unity, a disappearing unity."[5]

Debord describes this project of unitary urbanism when he explains "that the most fruitful numerical arrangement" for a *dérive* "consists of several small groups of two or three people who have reached the same level of awareness, since cross-checking these different groups' impressions makes it possible to arrive at more objective conclusions." One would hope that Debord's vision of teams of Situationists rushing around Paris communicating through walkie-talkies[6] would be at least in part an expression of a comedic imagination. But in fact he seems to have been quite serious about a new urbanism arising out of such a fiasco, so that the Situationist could "draft the first surveys of the psychogeographical articulations of a modern city," uncovering "unities of ambience, of their main components and their spatial localization" and ultimately pinpointing "psychogeographical pivotal points."

Lefebvre notes that Debord finally gave up this project, which is not surprising, given its contrived and abstractly intellectual nature. One finds a certain latent Cartesian rationalism in the Situationists' project that runs counter to their generally assumed commitment to the power of the radical imaginary. It's striking that in the theory of the *dérive* Debord gives few examples of what one *does* on a *dérive*, and no developed examples at all of what one *experiences*. As one of the slogans of May '68 said, "*À bas le sommaire!*"[7] Stop summarizing!

Yet, here's what we are offered: "Our rather anarchic lifestyle and even certain amusements considered dubious that have always been enjoyed among our entourage—slipping by night into houses undergoing demolition, hitchhiking nonstop and without destination through Paris during a transportation strike in the name of adding to the confusion, wandering in subterranean catacombs forbidden to the public, etc.—are

5. Interview with Kristin Ross, published in *October* 79 (Winter 1997); online at http://www.notbored.org/lefebvre-interview.html.
6. Or, in French, *talkies-walkies*. Perhaps this linguistic difference expresses the split between the Gallic prioritization of intellectual analysis, *talking the walk*, over the more practical but theoretically underdeveloped Anglo-Saxon *walking the talk*. The surregionalist takes along a *walkie-walkie*.
7. A collection of over 350 slogans of May '68, some with images and commentary, plus links to some excellent May '68 resources, can be found at http://users.skynet.be/ddz/mai68/index.html.

Workers and students fill the streets, Paris, May, 1968

Mai 68: l'explosion révolutionnaire. lcr-lagauche.be

expressions of a more general sensibility which is no different from that of the *dérive*. Written descriptions can be no more than passwords to this great game."

Particularly since hardly anyone was allowed into this *entourage* and most of those who were admitted were eventually expelled, this passage fairly drips with an attitude of "cooler than thou." But a few questions arise about the summary nature of this account: What precious gems were found in the rubble of the demolition? Why exactly should we look upon non-stop hitchhiking to nowhere as anything more than a moment in an obsessive *death dérive*? What mysteries were uncovered in the darkness of the catacombs? Why are all the passwords withheld from poor us, as if we are to remain mere spectators?

In short, why doesn't Debord give us something more than project proposals? Are we to conclude that the *dérive* is primarily a form of conceptual art? It's difficult to avoid the conclusion that Situationism[8] could not break adequately with the traditional standpoint of theory in which the theorizing subject stands in a position of dominance over the objects of experience, that despite its attempts at "critique of separation," its theoretical perspective remained trapped within the ideology of hierarchical dualism. Not to mention that slipping into condemned houses merely because there's a "Do Not Enter" sign and "Il est interdit d'interdire" ("It's forbidden to forbid") would suggest a rather

---

8. Yes, "Situationism." True, the Situationist International proclaimed in 1958 that "Situationism" is "a meaningless term improperly derived from ['situationist']," that "there is no such thing as situationism, which would mean a doctrine for interpreting existing conditions," and that "the notion of situationism is obviously devised by antisituationists." [See "Definitions" on the *Bureau of Public Secrets* website at http://www.bopsecrets.org/SI/1.definitions.htm]. But all this is far from obvious. What is clear is that such definitionism betrays a certain bad faith, unless taken ironically. As the Situationists knew well, calling something an "ism" often connotes that it is a sectarian tendency, possessing various dogmas and practicing various forms of exclusionism. This definition of an ism is what is intended in the famous anarchist maxim, "all isms are wasms." It's understandable that the Situationists would fear finding themselves dismissed as such a "wasm" and therefore consigned to the famous "dustbin of history." [N.B.: A "dustbin" is actually a "garbage can," though for some reason American leftists are uniformly incapable of that simple translation.] The truth must be faced: Situationism *is* a *wasm*, but it *was* an *ism*. Indeed, the Situationist International reveled in the agonies of its sectarian, ismic *jouissance*. According to one listing in a source sympathetic to Situationism, there were seventy-two members of the Situationist International, forty-three of whom were "excluded," and twenty-three of whom "resigned," some "forcibly." [See "Members of the Situationist International 1957 to 1972" on the *Not Bored* website at http://www.notbored.org/members.html] Situationism was an ism among isms in the annals of ismism!

superficial, reactive mode of rebellion.[9]

The Situationists expressed considerable contempt for what they saw as the failures of surrealism. Their critique of the obliviousness of most surrealists to its susceptibility to cooptation by the society of commodity consumption is precisely accurate. But the critique misses the point in its implication that presenting evidence of cooptation is a mortal blow to any movement or tendency. Is there any aesthetic, literary or political movement has been immune to cooptation by the society of consumption? Few of the Situationists have been around to see the extent to which Situationism and, of course, the May '68 revolt it helped inspire have themselves been co-opted. Have you gotten your *"Soyez réalistes: Demandez l'impossible!"* T-shirt yet? *"Prenez vos T-shirts pour des réalitiés!"*

I once went to an exhibit of works that a class of American students had produced after studying the Situationists for a semester in an art course. What was striking was the degree to which the critical edge of the movement had been blunted, as it had been filtered through forty years of history, the depredations of popular culture and dominant ideology, and, I assume, the ethos of the University and academic art study. A choice example was a poster that fairly accurately reproduced the *look* of a Situationist poster, but with the following text:

"The REAL terrorist is the college student who doesn't vote!"

Which, unfortunately, translates as "Be Realistic, Demand the Inevitable!"

Even worse is the cooptation of Situationism as part of oppositional lifestyle, or rather the image-of-oppositional lifestyle. An example is the trendy *détournement* of comic-book images, which, framed tastefully, go well on the walls of a loft, and make a distinct contribution to the urban ambience. In the end, *dérivisme*, though seemingly a form of *non-arrivisme*, can in fact become an advanced form of *arrivisme postmoderne*.

So much for *récuperation*. Nevertheless, the Situationists must be given their due for pointing out the extent to which surrealism was being co-opted. Yet, granted their prescient insight into the degree to

9. Greil Marcus, in his rather romanticized and dramaticized presentation of Debord and the Situationists, is able (justly) to make much of Debord's critique of the Spectacle, and at least something of his ideas of *détournement.* However, he can find little to say about the nature or significance of the *dérive.* See *Lipstick Traces: A Secret History of the Twentieth Century* (Cambridge, MA: Harvard University Press. 1989).

which surrealism would be integrated into the dominant culture, their general contempt for surrealism was badly misguided. Situationism for all its advances in the critique of the spectacle represented a regression from surrealism on the experiential level, and on the level of the creative imagination. For Debord, "the error that is at the root of surrealism is the idea of the infinite richness of the unconscious imagination," when in reality "the unconscious imagination is poor." One is reminded of Nietzsche's remark that when Kant proclaims that the dictates of his Moral Law are "necessary," this only raises the question of why they were necessary *for Kant*. One is tempted to conclude that the primary fact revealed by Debord's statement is that his own imagination is poor. However, this temptation should be avoided. What is, in fact, revealed is the abysmal separation between Debord and his own imagination, which despite his pretentions often manages to leap over the abyss.

As much as the Situationists are associated with *"l'imagination au pouvoir,"* Debord has a shockingly enormous blind spot in relation to the imaginary. He quotes urbanist Chombart de Lauwe to the effect that "an urban neighborhood is determined not only by geographical and economic factors, but also by the image that its inhabitants and those of other neighborhoods have of it." The fact that he feels a need to mention something so obvious—and to quote an authority in support of such a commonplace—indicates a naïve incapacity to grasp the centrality of the imaginary to the formation of any social reality. Such lapses seem to be related to the gap between his own vivid imagination and his goal-directed Prometheanism, which is accompanied by a fear of the anarchic powers of the imaginary that always subvert the ego and its projects.

Debord's own projects express a Promethean desire to subject the wild and unexpected to the dicates of the will. He explains that "if chance plays an important role in *dérives* this is because the methodology of psychogeographical observation is still in its infancy," and that "progress" consists of "breaking through fields where chance holds sway by creating new conditions more favorable to our purposes." As we will see, Deep Play, an alternative to the *dérive*, means forgetting all such progress, affirming chance (even if it is just an illusion) and denying that chance can ever "hold sway." It means putting aside our purposes at certain times. It means overcoming the obsession with creating new conditions, and allowing them to manifest themselves—in our so called "environment" and in our so-called "selves."

After expressing considerable contempt for the potentialities of "open country" and rural nature, which he seems to think of as mere boring, empty space, Debord points out "the primarily urban character of the *dérive*," which is "in its element in the great industrially transformed cities that are such rich centers of possibilities and meanings." In explaining why such environments are so rich in resources, he cites Marx's observation that "men can see nothing around them that is not their own image; everything speaks to them of themselves. Their very landscape is alive."

This statement illustrates both the brilliance and the limitations of Marx, a genius who suffered from periodical attacks of the idiocy of urban life. He is, indeed, absolutely right in noting that men, human beings, always shape the objects of experience in their own image (contrary to the naïve illusions of all ideological thinkers), but it is also important to understand that it is *men* who can *only* see what is in their own image. This is, in fact, the definition of a "man" and particularly "civilized man" as opposed to "human being." The child, entranced by the image and reality of the other, is still capable of Deep Play, finding in the other something that overturns all preconceptions. To grow up and be a "real man" is to forget this capacity (negating negative capabilities), to make oneself into the image of the Other, and then always to find ones own supposed image in the other.

One of the most disturbing aspects of Debord's quest for unitary urbanism is his view of borders. "Today," he says, "the different unities of atmosphere and of dwellings are not precisely marked off, but are surrounded by more or less extended bordering regions." This should not be surprising. Any deep experience of regionalities subverts the idea of distinct borders. Just as one is constantly discovering new borders or borderings, one discovers their relative and imaginary nature. Regionalities are continually defined and undefined by borderless borders, entered through gateless gates. But Debord sees the multiplicity of borders and bordering regionalities as an obstacle to be overcome. "The most general change that the *dérive* experiences lead to proposing is the constant diminution of these border regions, up to the point of their complete suppression."

Debord has a vendetta against the ordinary that blinds him to much of what the city has to offer. In his opinion, most of urban life consists of situations that are "so dull that they give a definite impression of sameness," and it is thus necessary to "try to construct situations, that is to say, collective ambiences, ensembles of impressions determining the quality of a moment." As usual, he reveals little about the nature of such moments, merely assuring us that "the powers of a situation will certainly expand considerably in both time and space with the realizations of unitary urbanism or the education of a Situationist generation."

He is, of course, right in bemoaning the effects of a regimented, bureaucratized, technologized, mediatized, commodified culture of economistic production and consumption. He is unquestionably right when he says that we must move "beyond the ruins of the modern spectacle." He is also right in his perception that few in his time (just as few today) see the degree to which the Spectacle degrades everyday life. What he fails to grasp is that human beings always resist the kind of reduction that he laments, and that they do so with a certain degree of success. They constantly "construct situations" and forms of self-expression that are diverse, creative, and astounding. Such forms pervade the urban landscape and are the subject-matter of surregional urban explorations. The city is a rich cultural ecosystem. Just as one finds much more biodiversity in a rainforest (or most other ecosystems) than in the results of a tree-planting project, one finds more diversity dispersed through the urban cultural ecosystem than will arise out of situations constructed by a cultural avant-garde.

It is appropriate but not without irony that Debord launches an attack on the heroic. He asserts that "the most pertinent revolutionary experiments in culture have sought to break the spectators' psychological identification with the hero so as to draw them into activity by provoking their capacities to revolutionize their own lives." This goal of breaking the stranglehold on the imagination of the Spectacle and its rich, powerful, famous heroes is, of course, an excellent one. However, the Situationist project in its Promethean moment itself succumbs to the snare of the heroic will to power. It is important to ask whether in the wake of seemingly revolutionary transformation the putatively liberated subject comes to identify with an internal imaginary hero that replaces the deposed external one.

This is another way in which the Situationist project subverts itself. Yet, despite all its internal contradictions, Debord's work remains of inestimable value, most particularly in his critique of the Spectacle, and *The Society of the Spectacle* remains one of those few invaluable books that can begin to shake the reader's faith that a ludicrously absurd and criminally insane social order must be absolutely equivalent to the inherent and eternally ordained nature of things.

There is also an important core of truth in the *dérive* that should not be overlooked, even while considering the many divergences from it. This is expressed well in an article on Debord by Pierre Macherey, who notes that the originality of the *dérive* is that it proposes that one "traverse a preexisting space, that of the city, while rejecting the conventional manner of doing so, and instead rediscovering it in strange and unprecedented forms, as if one were exploring a *terra incognita*."[10]

Oh, yes, beginner's mind.

Max Cafard

Make a spectacle of yourself.

---

10. Pierre Macherey, "Debord : Du Spectacle au Contre-Spectacle" in *Savoirs Textes Langage* (CNRS), 3/30/05, online athttp://tinyurl.com/ccbsevu (my translation). In this matter, as in all others, it is important to give Situationism its due. All fully-justified defamation in the present text notwithstanding, Debord's *Society of the Spectacle* is one of the most important books of the 20th Century and is required reading, especially for those culture consumers and devotees of "theory" whose acquaintance with it comes primarily from post-mortemist cliché-mongering and name-dropping popularization.

Chapel of St. Roch, Campo Santo, New Orleans.

Alexey Sergeev

2
DEEP PLAY IN THE CITY

The defining moment of our epoch was the moment when somebody decided that everything needed a defining moment. What we really need to find is the undefining moment of each phenomenon. The anarchist moment. The moment when it is liberated from our definitions and dominations and is allowed to reveal itself in its wild becoming.

The kind of play to be considered here is related, but is not identical to carnivalesque play. The carnivalesque disengages and liberates us from the rigidities of social structure, from the iron chains of oligarchy, from the sedimented layers of desiccated culture, from the zombiesque world of social autonomism. It does this through celebrating all that is neglected, disfigured and repressed by the dominant structures of society and selfhood. The carnivalesque, for all its creative affirmation, retains a certain moment of reactivity. This is not at all a bad thing, since it is the source of much of the passionate intensity of carnivalesque celebration and of its invaluable function as one of the highest (and lowest) forms of ludic critique. It reverses the Napoleonic dictum and proclaims: *"Le Pouvoir est toujours ridicule!"* Deep Play does all the liberating things just mentioned and more, but does it through a kind of engaged disengagement, an engagement with things themselves, that liberates us from each and every thing, even the thing called self.

Deep Play is openness to the experience of diverse, interpenetrating regionalities. We might think that when we engage in Deep Play, we are merely playing some kind of game, or even that we are pursuing some kind of game, that it is like a safari or a scavenger hunt for strange objects, which can then be exhibited in our dada collection, or used to expand our surrealist resume, or to add a notch on our Situationist revolver. But on the deeper level of analysis, Deep Play is not a big game hunt, nor is it playing a game in any usual sense. Rather, it is entering into the play of things, and the many interpenetrating worlds of those things themselves (for there is no *thing in itself*, only *things outside themselves* and *outsides inside themselves*). Deep Play is the interplay of psychoregion, mythoregion, socioregion, ethnoregion, bioregion, georegion, and all the other interpenetrating, mutually transforming regionalities. In Deep Play we enter into that interplay. If we want to think of it as playing a game, or hunting game, we must think of it at the same time as the game playing us, or playfully preying on us.

So what then is Deep Play in the City all about? It's about the Jewel Net of Indra in the Hood. You'll learn very little about it here. This text is not your neighborhood! There's no Thing inside the text.

Deep Play is close to what Daoist philosophy calls *wuwei*, an indefinable term usually defined as "doing without doing." Acting without the acting of an actor. Doing without the doing of a doer. It's also close to Zen mind, which has been described as "thought without a thinker." So when we go on a surregional exploration (of the city, for example), we take a tour without the tourists. It's a tour (a word that means "turm") of what is inside and outside. And just as when we breathe in and out, what is out is in and what is in is out. All of our experience is this turning back and forth of the inner and outer, exploring regions that are both inner and outer, and neither inner nor outer, and everywhere in between. The most widely practiced koan in the Korean tradition is "What is this?"[1] Deep Play is playing "What is This?"

In Deep Play, every object is a kind of koan. As the great New Orleans surrealist photographer Clarence Laughlin said, "Everything, everything, no matter how commonplace and ugly, has secret meanings. Everything."[2] The first step is to annihilate every thing's prefabricated

---

1. Martin Batchelor, "What is This?" in *Principles of Zen* (London: HarperCollins, 1999), pp. 83-86.
2. Clarence John Laughlin, "The Art and Thought of An American Surrealist," Interview with Clarence Laughlin by Patricia Leighten in *History of Photography* 44 (April-June 1988), p.72.

meaning, which means that we have to annihilate our preconceptions about it, our imposed purposes and projects. It has been said that the answer to the koan is in the life of the practitioner.[3] Responding to the koan means living the koan. Similarly, surregional exploration presupposes being alive, and requires dedication to living the things one explores.

Deep Play is related to the ancient cosmological anti-principle of *lila*, the ultimate play of the universe. *Lila* is the deepest play because it is prior to anything. It can't be *for* anything, because it comes before there *is* anything. Indian thought sometimes says it's the play of Brahman, the ultimate reality. But since it is primordial, it must play this Brahman too, rather than being played *by* it. It's also sometimes said that there's another Brahman beyond Brahman that is a Great Nothingness. Which in this case rings true, since real play has nothing behind it, no pretext, Nothing.

Clarence Laughlin, détournement by Stephen Duplantier

Clarence Laughlin Among Ghostly Mississippean Ruins.

If this seems too esoteric, we can also consider that this is closely related to what all of us call "play," the kind of play we reveled in before

---

3. For example, Thich Nhat Hanh, in *Zen Keys* (New York: Doubleday Image Books, 1995), p. 57.

we learned games and long before we learned to keep score. We still remember a lot about it, even if we haven't consciously done much of it for an unconscionably long time. So when we engage in Deep Play, in the city or elsewhere, we have to seek (through not seeking), or merely allow to return to us, this spirit of *lila*, *wuwei*, or child's play. This may not seem all that easy, for along the way we will find a lot to accomplish, so we will have to escape the temptation to get hopelessly lost and end up accomplishing it.

Deep Play takes place within the world's great gift economy. It recognizes that we we do not receive because we deserve anything or because of anything we do. It looks upon everything as gratuitous, as Lagniappe, the free supplement. It's a little like those ads telling you that if you buy their product you get 20% extra free. But in this case, you just take the free part and refuse to buy the product. It's the extra that comes with Nothing.

The Road to Topia

"Deep Play in the City" is an experiment in TOPIANISM. *Utopianism* is the search for a higher, deeper or better reality in some other place. Or more precisely, in no place at all, but a no place that draws us on toward itself and impossibly creates itself somewhere, to some extent, along the way.

It cannot be denied that Utopianism has its place, or at least its no place. But if utopianism has been shamefully neglected, *topianism* has been all but ignored, and this is the much greater tragedy. There's a time and place for no place and there is a time and place for place. This does not go without saying. For as we know, for certain neurotics everything is always out of place. What is not always recognized is that these neurotics rule the world. For our neurotic civilization, place is always out of place. Its obsessive fantasy is to replace every place with a no place, an Atopia, that's a million miles from Utopia.

Topianism means simply (and at the same time very complexly) *being here*. Our peculiar kind of human existence has been called "Dasein," using a German everyday deeply crazy word, which, since "da" means both "here" and "there," itself means both "Being-Here" and "Being-There" at the same time. Most of us know the feeling. Our existence may in fact not have to seem that way, and it probably didn't until fairly recently, but it's actually a good description of late capitalist, late civilizational, spectacularized, commodified consciousness, which doesn't know where in the post-modern Hell it is at any given time.

Surregionalism proposes the alternative of "Dadasein," which dialectically posits the *da* of *da*, and ends up where it always was, *hier*. When we are fully here we are also fully there. Deep Play means being fully immersed in the thing that is here, and at the same time being fully absorbed in the surregional journey through which the thing takes us beyond itself and our selves. Topianism is this Dadasein.

The Topia that we seek in urban surregional exploration is the Dadaic City.

Makuse

Flotsam: the neglected phenomena of the ecology of the disregarded.

The Ordinary

Gary Snyder has said that "the truly experienced person delights in the ordinary."[4] Deep Play and surregional exploration are about having, without having, that kind of experience. Freud was once asked by a patient if he could cure her unhappiness, and Freud replied that he couldn't, but he could bring her up to level of everyday ordinary

4. Gary Snyder, *Practice of the Wild* (San Francisco: North Point Press, 1990), p. 153.

unhappiness (coincidentally, what society expects and needs from us to keep us producing and consuming optimally). This is not the "ordinariness" of Deep Play, which is based on the thesis that both everyday, ordinary unhappiness, and also some of the more extraordinary kinds, result precisely from a lack of deep experience of things ordinary.

Everyday life, as many Surrealists and Situationists have enjoyed pointing out, is one of misery, but this is true only because the accent falls so heavily on the everyday and not on the life. Thoreau said in a similar vein that "the mass of men lead lives of quiet desperation."[5] This was, of course, long before everyone spent most of their lives on cell phones. In a way all that has changed is that a kind of personal autism has been replaced by a more collective variety, while the desperation persists. Deep Play promises no sure-fire cure for existence itself but leads us toward a certain enjoyment through desperately seeking nothing, taking the ordinary objects of experience as extraordinary gifts, and delighting in what is given. As Laozi said, we shouldn't destroy our lives contending for conspicuously exhibited "rare treasures," while overlooking those that lie around us, obscured by their ordinariness. As Varahamihira instructs us:

> *The gold of poetry*
> *Gets smelted and refined*
> *From the speech of*
> > *Unreflective men.*
> > *Let us go*
> *Cheerfully among them*
> *With poised minds.*[6]

Franklin Rosemont expresses beautifully this spirit of the gift of the ordinary in his definitive work on the scandalously neglected topic of Wrong Numbers.[7] In his *magnum opus* of Misnumerology he explains that "in every Wrong Number, the present moment is not only isolated but also intensified by the unexpected; while it lasts, it is the sole focus,

5. Henry David Thoreau, "Economy" in *Walden*; online at http://thoreau.eserver.org/walden1a.html.

6. Andrew Schelling, trans., *Dropping the Bow: Poems from Ancient India* (Seattle, WA: Broken Moon Press, 1991), p. 45. Thanks to Gary Snyder for drawing attention to this marvelous, incisive passage.

7. Franklin Rosemont, *An Open Entrance to the Shut Palace of WRONG NUMBERS* (Chicago: Surrealist Editions, 2003).

the whole reality. Like poetry and love, the Wrong Number recognizes the present moment—the magical *now*—as the 'open sesame' of freedom, the Marvelous, the fulfillment of our wildest dreams."[8] What we seldom realize is that the vast majority of Right Numbers are existentially and experientially wrong, since they are excruciatingly and deadeningly predictable. It is the Wrong Number that has the ring of truth.

But hung up as we are on rightness, we hang up much too quickly on the wrong ones (the *odd* numbers and *irrational* numbers in every sphere), with all their striking absurdities and sublime revelations. Why is one of the most hated characters in our contemporary abrasive society the miscreant who mistakenly phones us and hangs up on *us* in annoyance? On a superficial level, it's because of the culprit's bad manners. But on a deeper metaphysical level it's because this reprobate ruthlessly negates the entire mystery of our being (and thereby stands in for the entire social order of the crushing Megamachine and its insensate Technocracy that carries this out on the larger scale). One wonders whether such a person is capable of paying attention when it's the *right* number, in any sense of the term.

The "playful science of wrong numbers" is, as we see, an indispensible sphere of inquiry that yields many unexpected rewards. But as Rosemont notes, it is also significant because it is "part of a larger science of neglected phenomena of all kinds," part of the "ecology of the disregarded."[9]

The Endotic

Another way of putting this is that surregional exploration, and perhaps especially urban surregional exploration, is concerned with the *endotic*, as opposed to the *exotic*. Conventional wisdom links the exotic to sophistication. But this wisdom is sophism. Often it is precisely one who is inexperienced in the most vital sense who seeks to delude others (and perhaps him or herself) through exoticism. The exotic signifies literally that which is from outside. The outside and outsiders are crucial, and they are most crucial when they cross the all-important, non-existent boundary and enter into the inside, overturning all the conventional ideas of inside and outside.[10]

But the mystique of the exotic is not related to the outside that

---

8. Ibid., p. 145.
9. Ibid., p. 151.
10. See Andrei Codrescu, *The Disappearance of the Outside: A Manifesto of Escape* (Reading, MA: Addison-Wesley, 1990).

challenges the limits of the inside by inhabiting it, uncovering its secrets, and perhaps subverting it or forcing it to be what it longs to be. Rather, the exotic outside retains an inert externality. The allure of the exotic object depends on maintaining a split between imagination and experience. That object subsists in a world of abstraction and loses its alluring qualities to the extent that it begins to be known more deeply and intimately, that is, the way the endotic is known. Endoticism focuses on the Thusness of things, their being-here, while exoticism requires that they always dwell in some exclusive, inaccessible, mystifying There.

Georges Perec, in "Approches de quoi?" describes his approach to the endotic as a concern with "what happens everyday, the banal, the quotidian, the evident, the common, the ordinary, the infra-ordinary, the background noise, the habitual" and with the questions "how can

Jazz musicians mural, Parish Prison. New Orleans.

one account for it, how can one question it, how can one describe it?"[11] The surregionalist concept of the endotic is similar to Perec's, except that surregionalism does not have much interest in "accounting" for endotic realities, and it takes a more dialectical approach to these phenomena. It

11. Quoted in Anna Botta, "The *Alì Babà* project (1968-1972): Monumental History and the Silent Resistance of the Ordinary" in *Proceedings of the International Conference: The Value of Literature in and after the Seventies: The Case of Italy and Portugal*; online at http://congress70.library.uu.nl/index.html?000003/index.html.

is concerned not only that we focus intently on the evident, the common, and the ordinary, and allow them to reveal what they are, but also that we be open to finding the unexpected in the evident, the unique in the common, and the extraordinary in the ordinary. And that we explore the ways in which all of these things both are what they are not and are not what they are. We must be ready to discover that they all lead beyond themselves into other worlds, other regions of being and experiencing.

The passion for the ordinary and endotic is the practical negation of civilization's hierarchical dualism, which is founded on a heroically futile quest for a mythical ideal perfection, and in which everything can be ranked as higher or lower according to its relation to this abstract ideal, ranging from the most lowly, insignificant, ordinary, endotic (the unfortunately real), to the most perfect, extraordinary, exotic, powerful, godlike (the triumphantly illusory). Surregional exploration revels in the imperfection of things, in their being merely what they are. They are all ephemeral, flawed, and incomplete—in short, they are part of the real world rather than a product of fantasy. They are valuable precisely because they are part of the beautiful, broken, and sad world.

This is what Zen aesthetics conveys through the concept of *wabi-sabi*. *Wabi-sabi* refers to "the beauty of things imperfect, impermanent and incomplete" and "of things modest and humble."[12] It is "the exact opposite of the Western ideal of great beauty as something monumental, spectacular and enduring. *Wabi-sabi* is about the minor and the hidden, the tentative and the ephemeral: things so subtle and evanescent they are invisible to vulgar eyes."[13]

It's a *wabi-sabi* world and surregional exploration is about discovering the beauty, truth, goodness, and sometimes even the very existence of the small, humble, unfinished things that surround us, things and qualities that usually remain hidden just beyond our focus of attention. It's about putting aside our presuppositions and waking up to these unpresupposing and luminous things. No one said it better than Leonard Cohen:

> *There's a crack in everything*
>
> *that's how the light gets in.*"[14]

---

12. Leonard Koren, *Wabi-Sabi for Artists, Designers, Poets & Philosophers*. (Berkeley, CA: Stone Bridge Press, 1994), p. 7.
13. Ibid., p. 50.
14. Leonard Cohen, "Anthem."

The Surregional Object

Though descriptions necessarily address either one side or the other of this indivisible process, surregional exploration always *reveals both the depth of the thing and the beyond of the thing*. Breton writes of "the integral certainty produced by the emergence of a solution"[15] that one experiences when the Thing reveals itself in all its luminosity. The Surregional Object is such a Thing in that it is revelation that yields "certainty." But this certainty is the being of "a certain something," of a Thusness, a certain particularity that leads beyond itself, to a certain beyond, that is, a quite particular beyond. It is a solution that presents many further problems, an answer that poses an endless chain of further questions. Surregional objects are also "solutions" in that they dissolve our preconceived notions of things. They dissolve every thing, if they are not themselves dissolved in the "icy water of egoistical calculation."

They dissolve every thing, including themselves, in the sense that in exploring them not only do we discover Things but we also find that there are really no things, that each Thing leads us into a multitude of regions that give it meaning, that generate its thinghood and its nothinghood, that spawn uniqueness, specificity and Thusness, and also at the same moment lead all things outward into an infinitude of directions, and into an infinity of other realities that are not ultimately other. Determination is negation, so we must be determined to follow that negation wherever it leads. This is part of the meaning of meditating on Mu, "No!" or "Nothing!" The power of absolute negation propels us positively forward through "the Ten Thousand Things," so that as Zhuangzi said, we can stop struggling against the way of things and learn to ride the wind.

The Thing, the surregional, ultimately non-existent, noumenal object has something in common with Breton's *trouvaille*. Breton says that "what is delightful here is the dissimilarity itself which exists between the object wished for and *the object found*."[16] This is an enormously significant point. Surregional exploration (like surrealist exploration in its most uncorrupted form) subverts the civilized. The psychology of the surregional, wild object is the opposite of the psychology of the civilized object. The civilized object always produces frustration and a sense of

---

15. André Breton, *Mad Love*, trans. Mary Ann Caws (Lincoln, NE: University of Nebraska Press, 1987), p. 13.
16. Ibid.

lack because of the necessary gap between that object and the object wished for. (This is also called "sarvam dukham.") The wild object is the object of play, so it cannot be wished for. It is necessarily a surprise, a gift, and a revelation.

The term "object" comes from the roots meaning "to throw" and "toward." It thus seems to imply an intentionality and movement in the direction of some thing. But paradoxically, and dialectically, the "ob" of the "object" has come to mean also a reversal of direction, and thus a movement *away* from some thing, a being-moved of the subject. So we become the object's object. We may seek to "have" some object but once we are in the presence of that object, in its force field, perhaps we should say, it has us much more than we can possibly have *it*.

The Tathatic City

As we discover, the Dadaic City is also the Tathatic City. In all surregional exploration we seek the Thusness of things, their *tathata*. Han Shan, over a millennium ago, thought of this kind of exploration as a kind of tathatic *dérive*. As he says in the *Cold Mountain Poems*:

> *Freely drifting, I prowl the woods and streams*
> *And linger watching things themselves.*[17]

"*Zurück zur Sachen selbst!*" Han Shan's brief lines sum up concisely the essentials of Deep Play. It is a truly free drifting in which we are carried along beyond the bounds of our own and the world's delusions.

It is a discovery of Things Themselves that becomes possible when we "linger" while "drifting," doing without doing. Han Shan's drifting was like Thoreau's walking, for as he said, "in my walks I would fain return to my senses."[18]

Gary Snyder shows us that we can also prowl the urban woods and streams, the great wilderness at the heart of the city, if we know how to look for the things themselves there also. As he expresses it in one of the great texts of urban exploration, "Walking the New York Bedrock Alive in the Sea of Information":

---

17. Han Shan, "Cold Mountain Poem 7," trans. by Gary Snyder, in *Riprap & Cold Mountain Poems* (San Francisco: Grey Fox Press, 1958), p. 43.
18. In one of his greatest essays, "Walking"; online at http://www.transcendentalists.com/walking.htm.

Maple, oak, poplar, gingko

New leaves, "new green" on a rock ledge
Of steep little uplift, tucked among trees
Hot sun dapple—

> *wake up.*

Roll over and slide down the rockface
Walk away in the woods toward
A squirrel, toward
Rare people!

. . . .

Drop under the streetworld
Steel squeal of stopping and starting
Wind blows through black tunnels
spiderwebs, fungus, lichen.

Gingko trees of Gondwanaland. Pictographs,

Petroglyphs, cover the subways—
Empty eye sockets of buildings just built
Soul-less, they still wait the ceremony
that will make them too,
> *new, Big*
> *city Gods,*

Provided with conduit, cable and plumbing,

They will light up, breathe cool air,

Breathe the minds of the workers who work there—
The cloud of their knowing
As they soar in the sky, in the air,
Of the Sea
Of Information . . . .[19]

Even in this excerpt from the much longer poem, we can see how Snyder's exploration attends to a multitude of phenomena from many realms, and reveals the dialectical interaction between these realms. We discover an urban and at once more-than-urban world of sounds, sight, feelings, sensations, geography, geology, biology, sexuality, ecology, psychology, history, economics, social relations, class, anthropology,

19. From Gary Snyder "Walking the New York Bedrock Alive in the Sea of Information" in *Mountains and Rivers Without End* (Washington, D.C.: Counterpoint, 1996), pp. 97, 100.

archaeology, architecture, the symbolic, the natural and the social, the atmosphere, ritual, imagination, technology, politics, and myth—to give a non-exhaustive list. As Snyder summarizes the secret of this walk: "wake up."

Bashō, another surregional explorer, wrote *haibun*, journal entries interspersed with haiku, that reflect a dialectic between nature, culture, history, and psyche. He begins "Narrow Road to the Interior" with the observation that "the journey itself is home,"[20] and he looked at all that appeared on the journey as a gift. In "the Knapsack Notebook" he describes a point at which he was overcome by fatigue and his burden began to weigh on him physically and mentally. "With each slow step, my knees ached and I grew increasingly depressed." And then:

> *Exhausted! I sought*
> *a country inn, and found*
> *Wisteria in bloom*[21]

He doesn't mention whether he ever got to the inn.

The City Seen

Sengcan (Seng-t'san), in the first recorded Zen poem (circa 600 C.E.), said:

> *To ride the One Vehicle*
> *Do not despise the six senses."*[22]

This is a good guide to surregional exploration. The vehicle takes us along the road, the path, the way—in the present context, the city street. If we don't have confidence in our six senses (the five conventional ones plus mind) the vehicle will get us nowhere. The tradition that gave rise to Zen says metaphorically of our mind and other senses that we live in a house with six windows. It also says that we're like a crazed monkey that is trapped in this six-windowed dwelling. A psychotic little primate that seldom looks out the windows but spends most of its time bouncing against the walls and wreaking havoc with the furniture. In short, the Third Chimp is a Sick Puppy. Stated more historically, this means that since the beginning of civilization, and for very good practical reasons,

20. Matsuo Bashō , *The Essential Bashō* , trans. by Sam Hamill (Boston and London: Shambhala, 1998), p. 3.
21. Ibid., p. 65.
22. Mu Soeng, *Trust in Mind: The Rebellion of Chinese Zen* (Somerville, MA: Wisdom Publications, 2004), p. 154.

we have created for ourselves a psychological pseudo-reality that is a weird blend of autism and mental hyperactivity. It is not coincidental that the vehicle has taken us precisely nowhere (Atopia again).

Deep Play means breaking out of the autistic fantasy world that we've

Stephen Duplantier

"Petroglyphs, cover the subways—
Empty eye sockets of buildings just built..."

lived in since the origins of civilization and domination, and allowing ourselves to experience the realities, the Things and the thinglessness, the Thusness and the regionalities that are the beyond of Things, that our six senses reveal to us.

One point of departure for sensory exploration of the city is the visual, the sensory realm that has gotten the most attention. New Orleans surrealist photographer Clarence Laughlin expresses important aspects of a surregional view of the object and the image in his idea of a *seeing* that dwells on the object (often in images of decay and deterioration) but also goes far beyond the visual object into other realms. The visual image leads into a multitude of regions, which Laughlin explicitly identifies as psychological and symbolic, and which are also implicitly social, historical, cultural, natural, and metaphysical. He says,

> *I have tried to deal in an integrated and comprehensive*
> *fashion with the psychic significance of the multiple and*

> *often discordant forms that are found in the city of New*
> *Orleans, the time growths that completely render visible*
> *the psychological patterns of the era which evolved them*
> *(whatever that era may happen to be), [and] everything*
> *that embodies the spirit of 'place' or that indicates the*
> *meaning of a region at a particular period of time. . .*
> *This is symbolic photography.*[23]

Laughlin says that from the photographer's "intensive seeing" there "emerges a *surreality* which definitely transcends the purely recording function of the camera. The surreality consists of the extension of the individual object into a larger and more significant reality—the submarine depths and fantastic jungles of psychological association and symbolic meaning."[24] Surregionalism makes explicit the dimensions implicit in Laughlin's account and broadens the exploration, above all by shifting the focus more in the direction of the object, so that the revelation is less a one-sided psychological and symbolic revelation of the subject (individual or collective) through the object, and more of a mutual revelation of the subject-object field, through the regionalities that pervade both.

In 1853 the Baron Ludwig von Reizenstein, a Bavarian nobleman and immigrant to the Crescent City, wrote his fantastic and phantasmagorical *Mysteries of New Orleans*, a rambling, utterly implausible, and captivating work that runs to more than five-hundred pages of astute observations and hallucinatory imaginings.[25] In the Baron's inflamed imagination, New Orleans contained more of the mysterious, the bizarre and the grotesque than perhaps any place on earth. Part of the practice of expecting the unexpected is to investigate the extent to which even in a post-modern age of cynicism and disenchantment a city can still contain mysteries, secrets, wonders, miracles, magic, the bizarre, the uncanny, and the sacred. *(continued on page 33)*

---

23. Keith E. Davis, *Clarence John Laughlin: Visionary Photographer* (Kansas City, MO: Hallmark Cards, 1990), p. 27.

24. Clarence John Laughlin, "First Principles of the Third World of Photography: The World Beyond Documentation & Purism" in Franklin Rosemont, ed. *Arsenal: Surrealist Subversion 4* (Chicago: Black Swan Press, 1989), p. 96.

25. Baron Ludwig von Reizenstein, *Mysteries of New Orleans*, trans. by Steven Rowan (Baltimore and London: Johns Hopkins University Press, 2002). There were three different "Mysteries of New Orleans" works from the period, one in German, one in French, and one in English, representing the three major literate populations of the city at that time.

Ghosts Among the Ghosts Along the Mississippi

Clarence Laughlin, détournement by Stephen Duplantier

Ruins of Windsor Plantation, an African slave named Jack

Portfolio: A *détournement* of Clarence Laughlin's surreal photographs of Louisiana and the Mississippi delta with some overlooked elements added. Decanonizing Laughlin's imagery is the best legacy of his surrealist approach to symbolic photography.

—*Stephen Duplantier*

Clarence Laughlin, détournement by Stephen Duplantier

Plantation gentry and an African slave named Renty

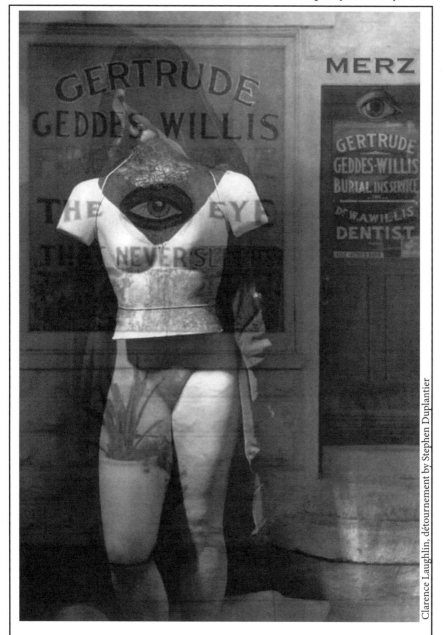

Gertrude Geddes Willis Funeral home, tagged with "Merz." New Orleans.

Clarence Laughlin, détournement by Stephen Duplantier

Hand on wall, woman in black, empty mausoleum, added hand of Jack Heartfield

Clarence Laughlin, détournement by Stephen Duplantier

Some of these mysteries are documented in *Geopsychic Wonders of New Orleans*,[26] which, like Laughlin's work, begins with the visual but probes far beyond it. A milestone in the history of the surregional exploration of New Orleans, the work combines the inspired efforts of geopsychical writer, critic and photographer Eric Bookhardt and hermeneuticist of the absurd Jon Newlin. It manifests acute, awakened perceptiveness, intimate connection with the local cultural milieu and history, a brilliant sense of the ridiculous sublime, and a deep love of place, all combined with a certain ironic distance that keeps it immune from the kind of idiotic puffery and cliché-mongering that plagues localism in general and Big Easy-ism in particular. This work opens the gateless gate of Creole surregionality.

Bookhardt and Newlin explore the "signs" of New Orleans and find them to point in strange and mysterious directions. "These signs," Newlin says, "are omens and portents." He describes "the sudden confrontation late one evening with a set of tile letters, embedded in the sidewalk of St. Claude Avenue near Poland Avenue, reading in a river-to-lake line of horizontals, Stop Don't Go Any Further." For Newlin, this "prompts two questions, For whom is this intended? Is it command or warning or both?" The sign can be taken as a koan, and if so performs a similar function as the koan "Mu." We must just keep in mind that we will find many other urban koans or signs that tell us "Don't stop!" and "Always Go Further!"

The Saturn Bar is the ultimate New Orleanian surregional social space, site of one of the most intense condensations of regionalities.

> *The ceiling—a mummy, elderly ceiling fan with dusty blade, a panorama of the galaxy and paintings nailed to the ceiling—there are paintings everywhere in the Saturn (subaqueous scenes, bullfights, swamp scenes, horses in pastures, postcard vistas of all climes, a beggar-thin hand throwing snake-eyes (with a Brueghelian tableaux beneath a shark about to gobble a smaller fish), cemetery scenes, symbolic portraits that might have been dreamed up by a cockeyed Redon); what is beneath the ceilings is no less bizarre—an Escorial of the bibelot—madonnas made entirely of glitter, a sea turtle mounted on the*

---

26. D. Eric Bookhardt and Jon Newlin, *Geopsychic Wonders of New Orleans* (New Orleans: Temperance Hall, Ltd., 1992; reprint of 1979 edition). The book has no page numbers.

wall outlined in neon with, across its shell, the alluring word
"Candy." Perhaps the most hallucinatory terrain for a cocktail
ever conceived, carried out ruthlessly according to one of the
most arcane Ninth Ward cosmologies ever to lurk beneath such
a deceptively, preposterously ordinary exterior.

The text is atypically restrained in its commentary on the remarkable
Chapel of St. Roch Cemetery. It evokes some significant aspects of the
Chapel's mystique in describing it as "an old-world scene of devotion,
fervor, immortelles and plaster casts of newly-whole physical parts,
reminders of physical transience."[27] But it is much more than this. It
is a powerful evocation of strangely intimate yet distant personal and
collective history, revealing links to a communal ancestry in Southern
Europe, evoking memories of ancient plagues juxtaposed with reminders
of the city's own history of catastrophic epidemics. Its atmosphere
is heavy with ambiguous nostalgia, and it shocks contemporary
sensibilities with its petrified remnants of a past era of devotion. It poses
a deeply ironic relation between past and present. And despite the ease
with which it can be perceived as a cultural curiosity, it retains a strange
and haunting beauty wrought by the ravages of time and now intensified
by the flooding in Hurricane Katrina of the Chapel and its neighborhood
(the neighborhood of my childhood).

A final example of an exploration of diverse regionalities that takes
the visual as the point of departure is the work of New Orleans artist
and ecologist of the imagination Jacqueline Bishop. She is best known
for her strikingly powerful rain forest paintings, raging from apocalyptic
Amazonian landscapes of fiery destruction and lush regeneration to
minutely detailed and sensuously numinous orchids.[28] But many of
her works emerge in part from the city and incorporate found objects
that she collects in early morning walks through the streets of New
Orleans. In some cases, the objects themselves become her canvas,
as in an extensive series of paintings on discarded baby shoes. She
says that "most people ignore or separate themselves from discarded

27. Many excellent St. Roch cemetery scenes can also be found online at http://www.
asergeev.com/pictures/archives/compress/2006/525/23.htm. These are from a remarkable
collection of 2254 images of New Orleans from 2005 and 2006 by Alexey Sergeev,
a physicist interested in "quantum-mechanical perturbation theory, summation of
divergent perturbation series, quasiclassical methods for resonant states." Extensive St.
Roch scenes of varying quality can be found at http://tinyurl.com/7zvtg8t.
28. An extensive collection of images of Bishop's work can be found on the Arthur Roger
Gallery site at http://www.arthurrogergallery.com/dynamic/artist.asp?artistid=7.

objects on the street, which are considered unwanted, used, dismissed and abandoned." They are not only ordinary, but as discards they are even sub-ordinary. For her, they are aesthetic, cultural and historical objects, works of nature and art that can be perceived and appreciated for what they are and what they embody, and also for the ways in which they can be incorporated in further generation of form, meaning and value. In Bishop's aesthetic, the creative process is a dialectic between several levels of preexisting meanings and forms and newly generated meanings and forms. She writes in an artist's statement,

> *As an artist I feel a mystery in the objects I find in the streets, for example, baby shoes, keys, nails, screws, door handles, human hair in the form of dreadlocks, silk ribbon and broken earrings, knowing they were used in a meaningful way by some human being I may never know. Collecting these objects and using them in my work is transforming them into another life, giving them another meaning.*

In a project with college students called "Discarded in Kentucky" the students "investigated the streets and each collected a specific, discarded object that would be considered garbage, abandoned, something discarded, rubbish, rejected, or what might be considered landfill material." Each student then "discussed the materials in this object (natural materials or man made; wood, plastic, paper, metals, steel" and his or her connection to this object or how he or she might identify with this object (cultural, religious, gendered, political, aesthetic)." Finally, each student "transformed this unwanted object into something else, giving it new meaning, a new existence, whether it be functional or purely aesthetic."

One of Bishop's most recent projects was a unique effort to help observers see what usually remains unseen, though it is right before their eyes. In a project called "Field Guide," volunteers used stencils of silhouettes of local native bird species to create five thousand images on a driveway in front of a complex of buildings that has been deserted since Hurricane Katrina.[29] The complex of buildings was once the Milne Boys' Home, a well-known local institution that is noteworthy in part because local music icon Louis Armstrong spent time there. The project calls attention to the abandonment of this site, which, like so much of

---

29. Images of work in progress on the project can be found at the Art in Action site at http://tinyurl.com/7hgn9ao.

New Orleans, including much of its population, has simply disappeared from collective consciousness, locally and throughout the United States of Amnesia, after the initial trauma and media bonanza of Katrina. But above all, the exhibit is for the birds. Five thousand birds may seem like overkill, but it is in fact about overkill, as the diversity of bird species in the region disappear from consciousness and then just disappear. It's an attack on oblivion and a wake-up call, with nature calling.

The focus thus far has been on the visual, but a large part of surregional exploration consists careful, conscious listening and hearing. Two large areas for such exploration of the city are listening to the noise of the city, and hearing the many voices of the city. John Cage said that "Wherever we are, what we hear is mostly noise. When we ignore it, it disturbs us. When we listen, we find it fascinating. The sound of a truck at fifty miles per hour. Static between the stations. Rain. We want to capture and control these sounds, to use them not as sound effects but as musical instruments."[30] Cage also said that "music is everywhere, you just have to have the ears to hear it."[31] Recent important explorations of both the Thusness of the music of everywhere and of musical regionalities include Steven Feld's "soundscape compositions" incorporating church bells, animal bells, and costume bells,[32] and, in a more urban mode, his recordings of the music, speeches, and sounds of the crowds at the Carrara, Italy anarchist May Day celebration.[33] Also of interest for their use of urban auditory source material are Quinn Kiesow's "Barcelona," "Madrid" and "New York."[34]

We will not run through all the senses here, but it should be taken as given that Deep Play will carry out its explorations through all of them, extending even to the most neglected and devalued of all, the sense of smell. Walter Benjamin has been justly recognized for his contribution to "the dialectics of seeing."[35] But the surregionalist non-project, its synject, will require not only a dialectics of this over-privileged sense, but also and *especially* a *Dialectics of Smelling*, not to mention a dialectics of all the other senses. Though surregionalists do not believe in self-

---

30. John Cage, *Silence-Lectures and Writings* (Marion Boyars Publishers Ltd., 2006), p. 3.
31. John Cage, "Anarchic Harmony," online at http://tinyurl.com/7ohj8he, and many other places.
32. Steven Feld, *The Time of Bells: Soundscapes of Italy, Finland, Greece and France* (Voxlox, 2004).
33. *Primo Maggio Anarchico: Carrara 2002* (FAI, 2003).
34. Online at http://tinyurl.com/7gjnyjl Less interesting is "L.A.," in which he explains it for NPR listeners.
35. Susan Buck-Morss, *The Dialectics of Seeing: Walter Benjamin and the Arcades Project* (Cambridge, MA: MIT Press, 1991).

identity, they are tempted to proclaim, "I smell, therefore I am," if only to give that most disparaged of senses its epistemological due, and to protest the fact that the onto-phallo-antinaso-logical tradition since the ancient Greeks has so discourteously and rather paradoxically snubbed, while contradictorily turning up, its nose at that very same humble organ, along with its scorned sense.

Granted, any American city is more of a challenge to the discriminating smeller than is, for example an Indian city, in which the fragrances of diverse curries and masalas, food markets, herb and spice merchants, perfumes, incense and thousand other scents reach out to the passer-by. Yet the smell of a crab, shrimp or crawfish boil in New Orleans is equally distinctive. As is the blooming of the jasmine, honeysuckle, sweet olive or magnolia. Yet there are thousands of more subtle scents that go unnoticed and remain for surregional investigation. But, however much we must attend to the specific phenomena, there is also a dialectic that encompasses all these visible things, audible things, tactile things, gustatory things, olfactory things, and leads us (as Laughlin emphasizes so strongly) to the most complex expressions of mind.

Surregional Lost and Found

One concise record of surregional exploration in New Orleans comes from an anonymous explorer in a message delivered not to the addressee but rather into the hands of fate (though perhaps the addressee will finally somehow find it here). The text and accompanying drawing were left on a table in the New Orleans Public Library. It reads in part:

20 March 1996 Day 3, New Orleans. Hello Elysabeth
I write to you from the city of great noises, the city of sweet smells, the city where all who move are Dancers. I walk these streets with wide open eyes, opened palms, and it seems that the creatures I see live inside-out. Insides everywhere, bursting and color-full. Time is present always and it is hard to erase. In this city the layers are raw and exposed. On houses, there are many colors, one beneath the other, scattered away with weather and storm and time and so much work it takes to live! Bricks and metal and wood, all showing, surfacing. Insides-out....

"...leaving records of their astounding discoveries scattered across the landscape."

When Deep Play comes to full fruition, the streets will be filled with anonymous surregional explorers, wandering through the Tathatic City, eyes wide open, allowing the outside to rush inward and vice versa, perhaps like Han Shan leaving records of their astounding discoveries scattered across the landscape.

Listening to the Secret Mind

In surregional exploration, the eye may be directed outward to the objects of vision, or it may be directed inward to the objects of mind. In certain very revealing cases, the eye focuses on what has passed through the eye of the storm, the storm in question being the tempestuous encounter with the traumatic real. What it discovers is the displaced perspective of the displaced, an anamorphic perception that is able to apprehend what could never be seen from the standpoint of the everyday, the stance of normality before the disruptive shift.

Such a traumatic encounter and such a process of displacement took place in New Orleans in the wake of the Hurricane Katrina disaster. They arose out of the loss of family, friends and neighbors, the loss of homes, possessions, and entire neighborhoods, and the loss of much of the personal and collective history of multitudes of people. The encounter with the impossible real can immobilize, but it can also liberate energies, and imagination. So along with the destruction and devastation, both external and internal, came an explosion of manifestations of personal and collective self-expression: a proliferation of internet archives, story projects, and photographic exhibits; a seemingly countless series of experientially-grounded documentary films; grassroots art and photography. The results of this outpouring constitute an extraordinarily detailed mapping of psychogeographical landscapes and regionalities.

Perhaps the deepest and most far-reaching of these explorations of the individual and collective, psychical and spiritual, imaginary and symbolic landscape of New Orleans is *The Post-Katrina Portrait Project*. Naomi Klein has written of what she calls "Disaster Capitalism," a monstrous system that preys on destruction, devastation and disorientation, and the "Shock Doctrine," its theoretical correlate, which stresses the vital role that collective trauma plays in expanding the parameters of exploitation. But there is also a Disaster Anarchism, and a corresponding Solidarity Principle, aimed at expanding the parameters of mutual aid, and these arise out of much the same dislocations. *The Post-Katrina Portraits* are in part a documentation of these phenomena.

Beginning a few days after Hurricane Katrina and continuing for over a year, Francesco di Santis drew portraits of a vast spectrum of people in New Orleans. This included Katrina survivors of diverse ethnicities, social classes, neighborhood backgrounds, age groups, and personal histories. It included those who stayed through the storm, the flood and the chaos that followed, and those who returned in the ensuing months. It included a vast array of volunteers—young anarchists and anti-authoritarians, global justice activists, idealistic college students, youth group volunteers, Rainbow Family hippies, concerned Christians, neo-Pagans, social justice workers, and heartbroken lovers of the city.

Di Santis asked each person to write his or her Katrina story on the portrait, or to tell the story so that it could be transcribed verbatim. In all, he did over two thousand portraits that contained over two thousand first-person accounts of experiences and reflections on the meaning of those experiences. Hundreds of them are collected online and hundreds are published in art-book format.[36] The Portrait Project is a profound and moving study of psychogeography, in particular the psychogeography of disaster and trauma, in which social geography is radically overturned, psychoregions are revolutionized, and long-obscured truths are illuminated by the clear light that shines forth out of the fissures in the contours of reality. For a moment, or perhaps

---

36. Online at http://postkatrinaportraits.org/ and with full resolution at http://www.flickr.com/photos/postkatrinaportraits/.

longer, the real surges forth and leaves traces that are often lost, but are sometimes retraced by a patient and revolutionary psychogeographer.

The *Portraits* is a record of alienation and righteous indignation:

> *You are looking at the face of a traumatized Katrina survivor! Katrina came and uprooted my family and community like a thief in the night. Been to so many places. You can never know what it was like for me and my child to see everything disappear right in front of our faces. The media lies! So did the people that told me they were taking me somewhere safe, but instead tossed us under a bridge, held at gunpoint without food or water for days on end.*

It is a record of the Dark Night of the Soul:

> *At night, it gets dark. Darker than I ever knew a city could become. Now the stars can finally be seen. Last night, I woke to the shaking of my room. The walls were rattling and the whole house moved. I clung to my bed. The earth was quaking and I thought, 'this is it.' Pieces of the world were coming apart and I tried to grasp onto the remaining fragments of reality—before it was all gone. I woke again.*

And a record of communal ecstasy:

> *I am in love. Completely, joyously in love. I have found my soul's match, my heart and mind's delight. I am in love with the people here. I have never been so continually inspired and amazed by the wonderful beings all around me. The volunteers whose skills seem boundless, their energy aflame, brilliant minds and spirits make me gasp with joy every day.*

It is a record of the horror of abandonment, as in these excerpts from a Katrina diary written on a marker board in the flooded Charity Hospital:

> *Day 1: We are all ok. . . .*
> *Day 2: We are all ok. . . .*
> *Day 3: Help is on the way. . . .*
> *Day 4: Where is the help? . . .*
> *Day 5: Bodies <u>floating in the water!</u> WHERE IS THE HELP?*
> *Day 6: WE ARE ALL GOING TO DIE!!"*

And a record of new realities surging forth from the breach:

> *What matters most is that within this system crack which*
> *was caused by Katrina we now have the chance to help enact*
> *a transformation of culture and civilization. . . . All points*
> *radiating out from this our swampy heaven. . . . all around me*
> *in this city I've seen art and music seeping up from the cracks*
> *in the hearts of people whose experiences and pain I can never*
> *understand.*

Perhaps these few short excerpts hint at the vast scope of the geographies of the mind and spirit that are mapped in this project. The message of the *Portraits* is epitomized in one of the shortest and most eloquent texts, which implores the reader: *"Open your eye, see what going on around you."* This is in fact the project of Deep Play and surregional exploration: to see with an awakened eye.

A certain kind of surregional exploration requires patiently wandering streets and alleyways, climbing rooftops, prying into neglected corners and abandoned attics, watching and waiting for what Cartier-Bresson called "the decisive moment," the surrealist moment in which the visual image condenses in our perception many levels of reality beyond the conventional one.

Another kind of surregional exploration requires patient tarrying with the people of a community, exploring every crack and crevice of their faces, every gleam or shadow in their eyes, listening intently to their stories. As di Santis expresses it, it means "receiving daily inundations of others' experiences as only the people who lived them could express," and in this way "entering a nuanced and beautiful reality" and "pursuing a sense of history or chain of events demonstrated by intense deliberations over single precious moments."

Significantly, di Santis notes that often the subjects "describe their acts and sentiments at decisive moments." This is Cartier-Bresson's surrealist moment in which levels of reality are condensed in perception, and it is the surregionalist moment in which what the artist calls "a simple loyalty to the present time" allows diverse personal, communal and historical regionalities to converge in an experience.

Not all psychogeographers can spend a year or more drawing thousands of portraits and collecting thousands of stories, but before they claim their Master of Psychogeography degrees they must first find their own unique variations of such an engaged practice. Though they may love quick kicks as much as anyone, they will never settle for a "rapid passage through varied ambiances." There is no Cafeteria of the Real. It takes numerous lifetimes to explore a city, but fortunately, if we slow down enough, we can live many of them simultaneously.

Urban Surregional Exploration: A Case Study

Debord gives as an example of a possible *dérive* itinerary, "wandering in subterranean catacombs forbidden to the public." This brings to mind a prime New Orleanian example of an urban surregional exploration. However, in near or below sea-level New Orleans, subterranean catacombs and caverns have to be situated at the superterranean level, unless one plans to do ones wandering in a submarine.

Each year at the conclusion of a certain celebratory event, a group of anarchic angels arrange a kind of celebration of the celebration, a meta-celebration, which is always held at a forbidden place, so that it can be what the most celebratory celebrations in a sense are, an exploration of various social, psychical and other regionalities that are commonly neglected, repressed or even forbidden.

What did the anarchic angels do in this case? What they did (largely without doing) was one part an act of imagination and ninety-nine parts a liberation of the spirits of the place, a letting be and letting do of those spirits. It was one part lighting candles to invoke those spirits and ninety-nine thousand parts succumbing to the powers of these anarchic divinities.

The local environment for this event was an eerie, deserted, slightly intimidating warehouse district in the dark of night. A chill autumn wind rushed through wide empty streets, vaguely illuminated by the dim yellowy glow of sparsely scattered streetlights. Large, blank-faced, monolithic structures lined the streets. In short, a more or less German expressionist setting. Very *M*-ish. Very disinviting, oozing vague angst and reification—an excellent dialectical contrast to what was to come. The specific site for the event was a huge, ancient abandoned power plant, towering above the surrounding structures, clearly marked "Keep Out."

One entered the mammoth structure through a small opening where a panel had been removed from the bottom half of a locked door. One

A meta-celebration held at a forbidden place.

Sarah Talffey, modified

Alexey Sergeev

"What did the anarchic angels do...?"
Angel with trumpet, tomb of jazz musician Louis Prima in Metairie Cemetery, New Orleans.

then passed through a small room that leads through a passage into one of the structure's vast superterranean caverns. There one found great expanses of space lit dimly by flickering candlelight that trailed off into complete darkness. Small votive candles were placed one on each step of the stairways so that they created a narrow pathway of flickering light that spiraled up into the heights. One then ascended the precarious stairways, and crossed over catwalks and high walkways, some without railings, to finally reach the roof of the structure.

A set of beautiful images of this power plant can be found online.[37]

37. Online at http://flickr.com/photos/talf/1573325354/.

These daylight images exude a strong *wabi-sabi* spirit of a place that has
been creatively transformed by the subtle, miraculous power of long
disuse, by the action of non-action. They present an astonishing contrast
to the rather overpowering, mysterious, almost sublime force of the same
spaces vaguely and evocatively apprehended by candlelight.

From the heights of the structure one discovered a panoramic view
of the skyline of the city, the nearby Mississippi River bridge, and the
river itself illuminated by the lights of huge cargo ships and tankers,
towboats, ferries and other vessels. The anarcho-angelic beings had
arranged for a large sound system to be transported to the roof. The
music, though powerful enough to pervade a large outdoor space in the
midst of a strong wind, was so distant from the street level that it could
not be detected from below. On the rooftop, one found a diverse group
of people, including artists, writers, musicians, poets, anarchists (angelic
and otherwise), travelers, and post-Katrina volunteer aid workers, in
addition to a contingent of dedicated party-goers. The edifice is crowned
by a huge smokestack. Some of the more intrepid explorers climbed it,
rather precariously, to some wooden scaffolding hundreds of feet above.

I left before the climactic ending, described by a Canadian anarchist:

> All was grand until the New Orleans Police Department showed
> up to raid the place. . . . It was a fairly surreal affair; lying on the
> gravel roof of an abandoned power plant at two in the morning
> with a hundred other folks while being berated by gun-and riot-
> baton wielding cops.

Despite the NOPD's reputation for excellence in arrests based on
fantasized offenses—symbolized by the mythical charge of "leaning with
intent to fall"—the police must have fallen under the hypnotic power of
some spirit, perhaps the locally-revered Goddess Eris, for no one was
taken in.

Illustration by Stephen Duplantier after M.C. Escher

3
SURREALPOLITIK

W hat is Surrealpolitik? Some assumed that the answer had emerged in 2003 when a historian reported a shocking episode. According to the report, anarcho-surrealists set up surrealist torture cells during the Spanish Civil War.[1] French artist Alphonse Laurencic, put on trial after the war by the Fascists, confessed that he had invented a form of "psychotechnic" torture. Fascists were imprisoned in small cells in which everything sloped at weird angles, walls were covered with bizarre colors and geometric forms, and the floor was littered with geometrical blocks. The inmates were forced to watch the eyeball-slicing scene from "Un Chien Andalou." Finally, the meaning of *le surréalisme au pouvoir*.

Not quite. The episode, though almost universally reported as fact, was an obvious fraud. Think about it. What would an anarcho-surrealist artist on trial tell his Fascist inquisitors? The truth? Hardly. More probably, he would turn the tables and tell the Fascists what *their* penalty would be if handed down by an anarcho-surrealist court. Twenty years of very hard cinema! A strong hint that the whole thing was a mocking fantasy is the fact that the dimensions of the cell, though crowded with surrealist paraphernalia, was all of 3 by 6 feet. The Fascists of Laurencic's fantasy-world must have been evil little Liliputians.

1. As analyzed in the Spring, 2003 edition of the *Fifth Estate*. See Don LaCoss's article at http://flag.blackened.net/liberty/anarchotorture.html.

After Guillaume-Benjamin-Amand Duchenne de Boulogne, *Mécanisme de la Physionomie Humaine, 1862*

Elicting an expression of terror from the mimetic muscles

So this promising case of Surrealpolitik turned out to be a hoax. Fortunately, however, there are several works that go a long way in exploring the momentous topic of surrealism and the political. Much of what follows are comments and reflections inspired—or provoked— by Michael Löwy's recent work, *Morning Star: Surrealism, Marxism, Anarchism, Situationism, Utopia,*[2] though several other important works that confront the question of surrealism and politics will also be discussed.[3] The primary rationale for this reflection on surrealpolitik is to recognize the depth of the surrealist roots of anarcho-surregionalism. As will become obvious, the focus here is also on defending the anarchistic basis of surrealistic politics and sometimes with demolishing Löwy's case for collapsing together anarcho-surrealism and Troskyism.

The Black Mirror of Anarchism

Any discussion of surrealist politics will focus on the inescapable presence of André Breton, and this is true of Löwy's book. The question of the nature of Breton's politics is therefore a central one. In answering this question, he quotes Breton's radically libertarian statement that "freedom is the only cause worth serving."[4] As Löwy formulates it, "an irreducibly libertarian position right at the heart of Breton's evolution" was combined with his "Communism" and Marxism.[5] This is certainly true of Breton, though more precisely, his evolution led him increasingly closer to the heart of his libertarian position and away from views that compromised that outlook.

The "Morning Star" is an image taken from Breton's 1944 work *Arcanum 17*. The star represents "revolt itself," which Breton calls "the only creator of light."[6] This light, he says, is discovered through the three paths of "poetry, freedom, and love."[7] The "Morning Star" is thus a heroic, inspirational image, though in a way a strangely traditional one.

---

2. Michael Löwy, *Morning Star: Surrealism, Marxism, Anarchism, Situationism, Utopia* (Austin: University of Texas Press, 2009).
3. Specifically: Franklin Rosemont's *An Open Entrance to the Shut Palace of WRONG NUMBERS* (Chicago: Surrealist Editions, 2003); Penelope Rosemont's *Surrealist Women: An International Anthology* (Austin: University of Texas Press, 1998); and Ron Sakolsky's *Surrealist Subversions: Rants, Writings & Images by the Surrealist Movement in the United States* (Brooklyn, NY: Autonomedia, 2002).
4. Ibid.
5. Löwy, p. 24.
6. Ibid, p. viii.
7. Ibid.

Clarence Laughlin. détournement by Stephen Duplantier

*Arcana on top of arcana. Laughlin's Abbess of Thélème
and Morning Star in the Black Mirror*

For it has been "light" that illuminated everything of value throughout the history of Western civilization from Plato's Cave, through the Siècle des Lumières, all the way to King George the First's "Thousand Points of Light" and beyond.

The radicality inherent in Breton's image shines through in the fullness of its radiant darkness when in 1952 he can finally say that "it was in the black mirror of anarchism that surrealism first recognised itself."[8] Surreality is not revealed when bathed in the beneficently cruel and harsh light of civilized rationality. It can only be found when one peers into the infinite abyss of darkness, negativity, and creative nothingness. It appears when one "tarries with the negative," or better, when one is violently tossed on the turbulent seas of negativity, battered by the waves of negativity, and thrown upon the dark shore, finally reaching the side of the other, awake to the fact that there is no "one." The "Morning Star" is, in fact, as we already knew, the Evening Star that plunges us into the Dark Night of the Solar.

The reference to "the black mirror of anarchism" comes from Breton's brief but absolutely crucial text "La Claire Tour," which is, in effect, his final political testament. It is a work that, unlike the vast majority of Breton's writings, is very difficult to locate in either French or in English translation. Löwy quotes most of the opening line, but passes over the rest of this enormously revealing text in silence. It's understandable that many would turn away from this dazzlingly dark truth. Breton asks, "Black mirror, black mirror on the wall, who's the most revolutionary of them all?" Breton is quite clear about what the answer is, and what it is not. And it is an answer that is suitably dialectical and paradoxical. One looks into the dark depths of the "black mirror" to find a revolutionary path illuminated by the "bright tower" of anarchism.

Breton concludes that when "a human ideal has reached the depths of corruption" (and we shall see shortly what led it into those depths), the only solution is "to return to the principles which allowed it to take form." When we do so in this case we "encounter anarchism, and it alone."[9] Thus, one must give up ones political illusions, one by one (as Breton himself did) until one finally "hits bottom" politically. And *au fond*, one reaches the foundationless foundation. "Anarchism, and it alone." Anarchism for Breton is "socialism itself," it is "the demand for dignity of humans," including "their freedom as well as their well-

---

8. André Breton, "The Lighthouse" at http://raforum.info/spip.php?article2408&lang=fr.
9. Ibid.

being."[10] It is an expression of the desire for a classless, stateless society in which "all human values and aspirations can be realized."[11] And as we shall see, it is infinitely more than this. He concludes that this conception of anarchism is one that "the surrealists make their own, without reservation, today."[12]

The Land of Innocence

In Zen (the practice of being radically awake), one of the most stinging indictments is to observe that someone's actions or reactions "stink of Zen." That means "it's getting old." In Zen, the idea is to have "beginner's mind," which is the child's mind, for which all activity is discovery, and everything is new. Surrealism, which in many ways shares this Zen sensibility, is subject to the same malady. Some surrealist games seem too much like surrealist games. Some automatism seems too automatic, in the mechanistic sense of the term. If we seek surreality, it's important that we never forget Heraclitus's warning always to expect the unexpected lest when it occurs we won't notice it. He probably mentioned in some lost fragment that we need also to practice "unexpecting the expected." Expecting the unexpected and unexpecting the expected are eminently surrealist exercises.

Psychical automatism, which emerged out of free association, means precisely being nothing like an automaton. It means finding that *automatique* and *autrematique* are one and the same (though at the same time many and different). It means following the way of the Ten Thousand Things, of the wild world around us and the wild mind within us, and finding that these paths break down the barriers between these two interpenetrating realms. It means dissolving the rigidities of civilized character structure to allow the world to reveal itself around us and within us. It means replacing the positive quest for domination and domestication with the negative capability to allow the wild to flow through us. It means practicing *wu wei*, doing without doing. Surrealpolitik is *Macht(nichts)politik*. It is the anarchic and surrealist politics of everyday life.

This is why Franklin Rosemont's *An Open Entrance to the Shut Palace of Wrong Numbers* is so enormously significant. It is certainly free of

10. Ibid.
11. Ibid.
12. Ibid.

any lingering odor of stale surrealism. It's no corpse warmed over. It's a product of the New World of Surrealism. This doesn't just mean "New World" Chicago as opposed to "Old World" Paris. It means, above all, the New World that is perpetually discovered by every child. It is a world of joy, spontaneity, affection, openness. Some might have difficulty deciphering the politics of the book. It seems like fun and games, child's play. Which is the whole point of the book. The child is the great sage. As Laozi said in his absolutely conclusive argument, "the child can cry all day without getting hoarse, and thus must truly be in accord with the dao."[13] And Rosemont quotes Breton's judgment in the *Surrealist Manifesto* that "it is perhaps childhood that comes closest to 'real life.'"[14] The quotes are presumably needed because he doesn't mean the unreal life that's usually called "real life," (the kind that "schools that work better" prepare you for), but the surreal life that is usually called "unreal." Rosemont's politics is the politics of eros versus thanatos. The true "Party of Eros" is perhaps a kind of Children's Crusade.

The title of the book is overflowing with implications. The "Open Entrance" question, the problem of "opening the door" is the most crucial one possible. And the "numbers" at stake are considerable. William Blake pointed this out some time ago. "If the *doors* of perception were cleansed every thing would appear as it is, *infinite*."[15] Infinity is a very high number. Rosemont makes it clear that the entrance is to a path to shared perception and shared infinitude; it leads in the direction of the enchanted community. It is an expression of our "desire for a new and deliciously different society—*a community without borders or boredom*, and with equal rights for the unexpected."[16] A noble cause that cries out for a movement worthy of taking it up. Defend the Rights of the Unexpected!

Radical psychoanalysis has told much the same story, as surrealists from Breton on have realized. Surrealism is the practice of free association, and surrealist groups are free associations of those practicing free association, whether in works of art, or in the art of living everyday life. Norman Brown pointed out that radical psychoanalytic politics is really all about eros versus thanatos, but surrealism realized or rather surrealized this long before word of it spread in the 1960's. Löwy mentions the importance of love to surrealist politics a number

---

13. *Daodejing*, Ch. 55.
14. *Open Entrance*, p. 149.
15. Willam Blake, *The Marriage of Heaven and Hell*, Plate 14.
16. *Open Entrance*, p. 163.

of times, but to be honest it always sounds rather abstract. Rosemont in his little section called "Love Above All" goes a long way toward making it concrete.[17] He gives actual examples of the meaning of the "land of innocence" to which lovers "escape" and one gets a strong feeling of what the marvelous or wondrous that emerges in the midst of the ordinary is actually about. We get a hint of what it might mean for whole communities to escape to the land of enchantment and begin practicing the Rites of the Unexpected.

Dishegeling the Dialectic

Considering the parody of dialectic that nearly everyone—ranging from analytical philosophers to post-modernists and post-ists in general—has turned into the conventional wisdom, it must seem shocking that surrealists would want to claim the legacy of *dialectical thought*. We're all supposed to know by now that Hegel foists a contrived, deterministic, rationalistic, logocentric, etc. "master narrative" on us. But how can so many who go on endlessly about otherness, multiplicity, polysemy and the death of the author not notice that there is more than one Hegel (and less than one Hegel)? The delicate work of dialectic is a "Wages of Fear" kind of job. No matter how carefully you try to get where you think you're going, you're almost certain to blow yourself up along the way. Any "master narrative" you might have in your possession at the time is simultaneously exploded. At one point, Hegel discusses a certain stage of Spirit's development that he calls "the Night of the World." It's a stage in which an image of Being is "stored in the Spirit's treasury, in its Night. The image is unconscious. . . . The human being is this Night, this empty nothing which contains everything in its simplicity—a wealth of infinitely many representations, images, none of which occur to it directly, and none of which are not present. This [is] the Night, the interior of [human] nature, existing here—pure Self— [and] in phantasmagoric representations it is night everywhere: here a bloody head suddenly shoots up and there another white shape, only to disappear as suddenly. We see this Night when we look a human being in the eye, looking into a Night which turns terrifying."[18] This is no armored Prussian marching to the monotonous beat of Thesis-Antithesis-Synthesis. These are the words of an inspired

17. Ibid, pp. 147-49.
18. Hegel, *Philosophy of Spirit (1805-06)* at http://www.marxists.org/reference/archive/hegel/works/jl/ch01a.htm.

philosophical poet of *radical imagination* and *surreality*.

This is the dialectical heritage of surrealism. The situationists said *"l'imagination au pouvoir,"* but the surrealists knew that the imagination is *always* in power and this could be either the most wondrous of things or the most terrifying. All revolution is a war of the imagination, and it always takes place on imaginary grounds. Dialectical thought and imagination do not aim at synthesis, but are thoroughly pervaded by ongoing contradiction and opposition. As surrealists perceive acutely, things are often just the opposite of the way they seem—and the way that they seem has the most astounding implications if we begin to think intently and deeply about this very seeming.

The craziness of dialectic is manifested in the very word that Hegel uses to describe what happens to things in a dialectical process: *Aufheben. Aufheben* is translated as to "negate," "preserve," "keep," "transcend," "cancel," "overrule," "raise," "raise up," "abolish," "elevate," "annul," "end," "lift up," "break," "merge," "override," "supersede," "reverse," (the ever-popular but incomprehensible) "sublate," and finally, "suspend," which is a fascinating word in itself, since it means both to *stop* something and to *continue* it. It's easy to understand why surrealists find inspiration in Hegel. Contrary to the slanders of plodding post-modernists, the dialectic has nothing to do with the ideology of Hegel (or Marx), any more than psychoanalysis has anything to do with the dogmas of Freud. The dialectic demolishes all ideology and all dogma. It really is the ruthless critique of everything existing (though the ruthlessness is really dialectical tough love).

The reality of surreality is radical reversal—things turn into their opposites or transform into things that defy all our categories of opposition. Once again, as dialectics theorizes and surrealism demonstrates, everything always is what it is not and is not what it is (though as the ancient negative dialectican Nagarjuna theorized and Zen demonstrates, it also neither is nor is not what it is). Hegel pointed out that the truth is the whole, but he also showed, sometimes in spite of himself, in his most conceptually disheveled moments, that there really *is* no whole, and even when there is a whole, there's always a hole in the whole. The (w)hole is an empty (w)hole.

Radical dialectic is the anarchic movement of mind and reflects the anarchic movement of things themselves, the circulatory movement of material things, living things, dream things, magical things, imaginary things, unimaginable things, fragmented things, hybrid things, mutating things, impossible things. Surrealism is radical dialectic in creative practice.

The Amourfous Community

Löwy cites Peret's admirable description of surrealism as being in the tradition of Schlegel's dream of "a borderless mythopoetic universe" that was "under the transfiguration of imagination and love."[19] For surrealism there is an intimate connection between passion and politics, between *amour fou* and revolution. For Breton the greatest poetic, creative, transformative, revolutionary myth is *mad love*, love that "encompasses all one's passion" and possesses "the power to regenerate the world."[20]

A borderless, mythopoetic universe

Here, Breton touches on an enormously crucial truth. We must "regenerate the world!" The great irony and absurdity of ideology lies

19. Löwy, p. 14.
20. Ibid., p. 17.

first in that it not only *distorts* reality but that it turns reality into its *precise opposite*, and secondly that it assures that the one thing that we *ignore* with the greatest determination is that which is *most important.* So that one thing we can't think about is that the entire web of life on earth (*zoe*) is disintegrating, that we are living in the Sixth Great Mass Extinction of Life on Earth and facing a global ecological collapse, while at the same time the entire web of communal life (*bios*) has been disintegrating throughout the history of civilization and is entering into its death throes. Minor details!

Thus, surrealpolitik must be a biozöopolitics. In fact, a problematic of social and ecological regeneration is the only sane basis for any politics today (which is why politics in general is thoroughly insane). It is not entirely surprising that the impasse of the dominant Left for almost a century has been its vision of Revolution without Regeneration. "Revolution" may describe the physics of the matter, but "regeneration" describes its natural and social ecology. So we need to draw out the full meaning of Breton's statement, more meaning than he perhaps consciously intended, when he said that surrealism proclaims such "mad love" with "the power to regenerate the world." And at the same time with the power to regenerate each other. In a deadening world of domination and alienation, our surrealism and anarchism can become primarily reactive, other modes of remaining asleep, new modes of militantism, in short, isms. The amourfous community must know how to seduce the susceptible and awaken them: "Into the ear of every anarchist that sleeps but doesn't dream/We must sing, we must sing, we must sing."[21]

The surrealist problematic is one of regeneration through reenchantment. Löwy describes surrealism as "a movement of the human spirit of revolt and an eminently subversive attempt to re-enchant the world."[22] True, but the other essential part of the story is that the surrealist forces of enchantment do not encounter a merely disenchanted world. For one thing, we are originally born into an enchanted world and that world always remains somewhere within us, a reservoir for the reemergence of enchanted surreality. Secondly, as Marx pointed out regarding the fetishism of commodities, the inhabitant of the imaginary

---

21. Bright Eyes, "At the Bottom of Everything." In which the narrator of this little story in song is apparently relieved to find out that at the bottom he is no one. However, the sleeping, dreamless anarchist is described as a "that," rather than a "who," and therefore has seemingly fallen, not to the bottom of things, but into reification.
22. Ibid., p. 1.

world of capitalism is surrounded by and pervaded by enchanted objects, those mysterious subject-objects called commodities. So surrealism is not only about generating processes of reenchantment but also about waging war on the imaginary battlefield on which contending enchantments clash. It is about launching the forces of liberatory reenchantment and disenchantment all at once. Casting the spell of the surreal requires breaking the spell of spectacle, the enchanting consumptionist sublime.

Liberatory enchantment can really only succeed through the *force collective* of the enchanted community. Löwy very pertinently mentions Peret's appeal to the maroon community, the *quilombo*, as the model of the anti-authoritarian community of solidarity.[23] In one sense, the post-modern or late modern condition is precisely a condition of universal being-marooned. Unfortunately it's in the involuntary sense of being stranded in *limbo* by a run-away ("hot," overheated, running-out-of-control) society. What is needed is a revival of the intense desire for marooning in the voluntary sense of running away to *quilombo*, on order to create the liberated community, to escape that same over-controlling out-of-control society. A famous May '68 slogan was "*Cours, camarade, le vieux monde est derrière toi.*" Today you need to run twice as fast, because post-modernity is chasing after you at twice the speed, not just snapping at your ass, but trying to swallow you whole. You need some *place* to which you can escape. You need some magic phone booth you can run into and dial the right *wrong number* that sweeps you away to surreality.

It's important to see surrealism as part of the great tradition of utopian communalism. Surrealism adds to the idea of the *intentional community* the even more important idea of the *absolutely unintentional community*, which is a challenge to the Prometheanism, the misguided rationalism, and the obsessive programaticism of the traditional Left. The unintentional community is the utopian, imaginary community that reaches out to you from the realm of impossibility and grabs you! And all those like you. It tears you out of the chains of deadening everydayness and pulls you into the creative unknown, just as it at the same time pulls itself into the midst of *life itself*, in all its density of being. In doing so, it incarnates utopia in thick, topian materiality. Utopia finds itself in the *topos*, in the richness of place, in the profusion of particularity, in the wonders of the ordinary, in the magic of things

---

23. Ibid., p. 11.

themselves. But, of course, *it* only does it if we do it.

Löwy touches on this radical, anarchistic surrealist utopianism. He points out that the Romanticist dimension of surrealism is a very expansive sensibility that encompasses revolt against the destruction and degradation wrought by industrial society, a nostalgia for "a lost paradise," a movement of hope, a war on capitalist and technocratic quantifying values, and a rebellion against the disenchantment of the world.[24] He recalls the fact that primitive magical practices, alchemy and various esoteric arts have been admired by surrealists for their "charge of poetic electricity."[25] So true! Living in surreality means being continuously shocked into recognition and being occasionally (and often, if possible) literally struck by bolts of non-literal lightning. Contrary to Lenin:

> "Communism" is not "Soviet power plus electrification." Rather, *Anarcho-Communism* (the only kind possible) is *"poetic power* plus, above all, *"poetic electrification!"*

The Indelible Stain

And speaking of Communism . . . . While Löwy invokes Breton on behalf of the compatibility between surrealism, anarchism, and Trotskyism, Breton himself eventually saw Trotskyism as an obstacle to the surrealist project in general, and to its alliance with anarchism in particular. In his considered view, he saw that anarchism and surrealism were from the beginning inseparable. Yet, he notes, they were separated. He asks: "Why was an organic fusion unable to come about at this time [in early surrealism] between anarchist elements proper and surrealist elements?"[26] And he finds three reasons. The answer, he says, is first that "it was undoubtedly the idea of efficiency, which was the delusion of that period, that decided otherwise."[27] This is the delusion that the precondition for aesthetic and political progress is the further unleashing of industrialism and the vastly greater consumption of material goods. This is a form of the economistic delusion that has captured the imagination of the modern age, including that of the most ostensibly oppositional movements, so that the latter become what the early (more

---

24. Ibid., p. 29.
25. Ibid., p. 38.
26. Breton, "The Lighthouse"
27. Ibid.

Illustration by Stephen Duplantier

The feminine side of Trotsky: An improvement through the digital eugenic addition of the face of Frida Kahlo

radical and critical) Baudrillard called "the Mirror of Production."

The second obstacle was that "what we took to be the 'triumph' of the Russian Revolution and the advent of a 'worker's State' led to a great change in our perspective."[28] A classic story: the lure of triumphant power and capitulation to Realpolitik. The Revolution is declared a success to be emulated everywhere just as reactionary elements gain control and the system of domination is reinstituted in a new guise.

28. Ibid.

Breton remarks that "the only dark spot in the picture—a spot which was to become an indelible stain—consisted of the crushing of the Kronstadt rebellion on March 18th, 1921. The surrealists never quite managed to get beyond it."[29] Löwy does not, however, even get *to* it. He does not mention this dark spot, this dark mirroring stain that stares back into the innermost depths of the political observer. Who is it that "crushed" the Kronstadt Rebellion? The commander of the Red Army, the high official who ordered the Kronstadt sailors to surrender or be crushed, was one Leon Trotsky.

Third, Breton mentions that "around 1925 only the [Trotskyite] Third International seemed to possess the means required to transform the world."[30] In the sequel, we discover that this International didn't make much a dent on the real world or any part of it, but rather sank into the murky abyss of sectarianism. In short, highly unrealistic (not to mention highly un-surrealistic) illusions about Trotskyism got in the way. Breton adds that "We are well enough aware of the ruthless pillaging to which these illusions [i.e., those concerning: 1) the technocratic hell of economistic efficiency; 2) the grotesque horror of authoritarian revolutions; and 3) the deadening mire of Trotskyite sectarianism] were subjected during the second quarter of the century."[31]

Perhaps we should look more deeply into this fascinating question of the intersection of Trotsky, anarchy, and surreality.

"Anarchists Must Be Shotsky"—Leon Trotsky (1921)

One could argue the surrealists who fell for Stalinism might be more easily forgiven than those who went Trotskyist, on grounds that if a surrealist sins, he or she should sin as boldly as possible. Why not go for the genocidal sublime rather than some second-rate authoritarianism? This is actually an awful argument, but one must still wonder where the attraction of the rigid, unimaginative Trotsky comes from. Stalin was a wholesale mass murderer, while Trotsky merely did it retail, as indicated by his nickname, the "Butcher of Kronstadt" (which comes from the days when he was advising his Red Army to "shoot" the anti-authoritarian Kronstadt sailors "like partridges"). Stalin owned the slaughterhouse while Trotsky was a mere shopkeeper, a petit-bourgeois *boucher*.

---

29. Ibid.
30. Ibid.
31. Ibid.

"Just Kidding."—Leon Shpasky (1938)

However, as everyone knows, Trotsky was forced to lay down his meat cleaver and go into involuntary retirement. Strange things happened. Löwy quotes Trotsky as writing, during his days of exile in Mexico and in collaboration with André Breton, the text *For an Independent Revolutionary Art*. In it they write that "Marxists must march hand in hand with anarchists" in support of "an anarchist ideal of individual freedom for cultural creation."[32] It's amazing what a good surrealist friend and a condition of complete political powerlessness can do to someone suffering from an acute military-industrial complex. If only Breton had gotten through to him a bit earlier! Imagine, for example, that instead of slaughtering the Kronstadt rebels, Trotsky would have given an order for his troops to break through the lines and not let up until they were holding hands with every revolutionary sailor and doing something culturally creative. What a vast improvement over the Revolution, Bolshevik style!

It's hard to believe that Trotsky was serious about trotting over to surrealism, much less allying himself with the anarchists (apart from the fact that he was always deadly serious about everything). As Nick Heath comments about the "contradictory and bizarre document" he coauthored with Breton, "it is not clear when Trotsky helped write [it] what he thought he was doing, as it went against everything he had ever done or said."[33]

Pacify Nature!

Löwy makes a heroic effort to find libertarian and visionary impulses in an intellect that was authoritarian and rigid on the one hand, and plodding and pedestrian on the other. Take, for example, Trotsky's "vision of humanity." In his view, "man is a fairly lazy animal."[34] Don't think that this was a radical defense of the "right to be lazy" and the immediate utopian *dépassement* of the division between work and play. Quite to the contrary, Trotsky uses the human laziness premise to justify a reductionist, economistic, productionist vision of social evolution.

---

32. Löwy, p. 25.
33. http://libcom.org/history/1919-1950-the-politics-of-surrealism.
34. Leon Trotsky, *Terrorism and Communism*, Ch. 1, at http://www.marxists.org/archive/trotsky/1920/terrcomm/ch08.htm.

The great virtue of laziness, he reveals, is that it demands "the largest possible quantity of products in return for a small quantity of energy."[35] So it's "a progressive force"[36] in driving industrialism and technological development. Trotsky did have some minimal utopian potential, but to realize it he would probably have needed an extended stay in one of those dadaosurrealist prisons/fun houses set up (mythologically) by the Spanish anarchists.

On the other hand, his dystopianism was rather highly developed. His writings are littered with references to the need to "conquer" whatever is wild and free and "subject" it to rational control and triumphant will. Trotsky was not a wild and crazy guy. He was more on the domesticated and neurotic side. He feared what was wild and crazy. Whereas surrealism takes its stand on behalf of the wild, for Trotsky, authentic "culture" is a process of murdering it. Culture is the cult of domination. He defines it as "all kinds of knowledge and skill in the struggle with nature in order to pacify nature."[37] But it was one particular part of nature, human nature, that he was most interested in domesticating.

Is the New Man Having Fun Yet?

While surrealism thrives on making people feel uncomfortable, indeed, on smashing the zombifying state of comfort, Trotsky contends that "art needs comfort."[38] He almost stumbles inadvertently on the truth when he says that its precondition is "abundance."[39] But he doesn't mean the abundance that lurks behind the murderous illusion of scarcity first imposed by early civilization and finally perfected by late capitalism. No, for the kind of abundance that Trotskyite art needs, "furnaces have to be hotter, wheels have to move faster, looms have to turn more quickly, schools have to work better."[40] In other words, it needs what Breton epitomized as the delusion of "efficiency." But surrealist art has never needed any of this:

---

35. Ibid.
36. Ibid.
37. Leon Trotsky, "Culture and Socialism" at http://www.wsws.org/articles/2008/oct2008/cult-o23.shtml.
38. Leon Trotsky, "Literature and Revolution" at http://www.marxistsfr.org/archive/trotsky/1924/lit_revo/intro.htm.
39. Ibid.
40. Ibid.

Surrealist art needs nothing!
It desires everything!
The most excruciating comfort!
An abundance of lack!
The iciest of furnaces!
Wheels moving at infinite velocity going nowhere!
Looms instantaneously reweaving the world!
Schools that have nothing to do!
And do it with absolute perfection!

Meanwhile, back in dystopia. . . . Trotsky predicts that "socialist art will revive tragedy. Without God, of course. The new art will be atheist. [Dear Sophocles, I regret to inform you . . . .] It will also revive comedy, because the new man of the future will want to laugh."[41] Unfortunately, the laugh of "the new man," Trotsky's new guy of the future, will always be somewhere in the future, but Trotsky does give us a good laugh now. Maybe socialist art will revive porn because this new guy of the future needs orgasms. The Ministry of Orgasms will work it out. Troubling question: how does Trotsky know that this new guy of the future might not want mystical experiences? Is there room in the future for a Ministry of Gods? No doubt it could even provide atheist gods for people like Trotsky, in case some new guy of the future is like him.

Trotsky's aesthetic Five Year Plan (or was it Fifty? or Five Hundred?) is in a sense quite wonderful, surpassed only perhaps by "Plan 9 From Outer Space." He predicts that we humans will get off our lazy asses and begin to emulate the harmonious rhythms of those marvelous machines that our lazy-ass qualities originally made possible. "Man at last will begin to harmonize himself in earnest. He will make it his business to achieve beauty by giving the movement of his own limbs the utmost precision, purposefulness and economy in his work, his walk and his play."[42] It's easy to see why Emma Goldman didn't invite Leon to her revolution where everybody gets to dance. Can you imagine doing the Trotsky? The band Devo has done a number of videos addressing the dialectical contradictions inherent in this project.

---

41. "Introduction" to *Literature and Revolution* at http://www.marxistsfr.org/archive/trotsky/1924/lit_revo/.
42. "Revolutionary and Socialist Art" in *Literature and Revolution* at http://www.marxistsfr.org/archive/trotsky/1924/lit_revo/ch08.htm.

Master Digestion!

For surrealists, the unconscious is the source of creative inspiration and utopian imagination and must be liberated from the fetters of civilized repressive rationality and patriarchal repressive will. For Trotsky, the unconscious is a dangerous menace that needs to be "mastered" by the powers of rationality and will. "Man," he says "will try to master first the semiconscious and then the subconscious processes in his own organism, such as breathing, the circulation of the blood, digestion, reproduction, and, within necessary limits, he will try to subordinate them to the control of reason and will."[43] Breton defined surrealism in part as "Psychic automatism . . . . Dictated by the thought, in the absence of any control exercised by reason"—a view that is rather precisely the opposite of Trotsky's on the matter.[44] For Trotsky, we must look forward to the day when the proletarian masses have finally mastered their unconscionably unconscious blood circulation, and gotten those unruly "reproductive processes" under the control of will and reason. Then they will proclaim the great revolutionary watchword, "Master Digestion!" We're along way from "Take your desires for realities," not to mention "l'Amour Fou."

In the inadvertent dystopian science fiction story that Trotsky has written, "even purely physiologic life will become subject to collective experiments."[45] He predicts that "the human species, the coagulated *Homo sapiens*, will once more enter into a state of radical transformation, and, in his own hands, will become an object of the most complicated methods of artificial selection and psycho-physical training."[46] One can well imagine. "Object?"—definitely. "In our own hands?"—highly unlikely. One of our revolutionary tasks needs to be keeping the *Ministry of Psychophysical Experimentation*'s hands off us. No thanks, Leon, we can uncoagulate ourselves!

Superman, If You Please

In Trotsky's scientistic, technocratic view of history, "Man first drove the dark elements out of industry and ideology, by displacing barbarian

---

43. Ibid.
44. *Surrealist Manifesto* (1924) at http://wikilivres.info/wiki/Surrealist_Manifesto.
45. "Revolutionary and Socialist Art."
46. Ibid.

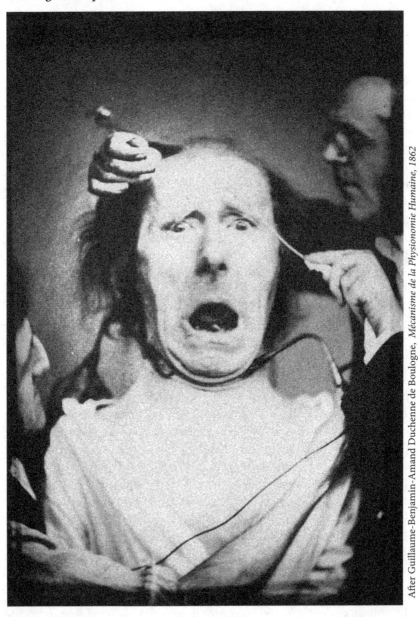

After Guillaume-Benjamin-Amand Duchenne de Boulogne, *Mécanisme de la Physionomie Humaine, 1862*

"...to extend the wires of his will into hidden recesses, and thereby to raise himself to a new plane, to create a higher social biologic type...a superman." —Leon Trotsky

routine by scientific technique, and religion by science."[47] So, according to Leon (alias "the Prophet") Trotsky, after another century of linear progress (maybe around 2012?), work everywhere will become something like ecstatic synchronized swimming, and all religion will have withered away, just like the state. "Man," he says, "drove the unconscious out of politics, by overthrowing monarchy and class with democracy and rationalist parliamentarianism and then with the clear and open Soviet dictatorship."[48] So Trotsky thought that the unconscious had been "driven out of politics" by 1924 when he was writing this book, which was published (consciously, we can assume with confidence) by the Soviet State. Trotsky certainly qualifies as one of the great (though quite *unconscious*) disclosers of the meaning of repression and the return of the repressed. Once more we see how "the sleep of rationalists breeds monsters." Very shortly, the Monster, in the form of Stalin, would venture forth to wreak havoc. But if Stalin had not existed, the unconscious would have found it necessary to create him. Some other Frankenstein or Borenstein Monster would certainly have arisen.

While surrealism is above all the poesis of freedom, Trotskyism is beneath it all a discourse of domination. Well, not that far beneath. In fact, Trotsky is quite explicit about his insanely rationalistic dream of domination, including the most insidious form of domination possible, *l'autodétournement*, the auto-cooptation of one's own stupid selfhood into the project of domination. "Man," he says, "will make it his purpose to master his own feelings, to raise his instincts to the heights of consciousness, to make them transparent, to extend the wires of his will into hidden recesses [yes, we'll even *wire* ourselves!], and thereby to raise himself to a new plane, to create a higher social biologic type, or, if you please, a superman."[49] Look! Up in the sky, in the heights of consciousness! It's a bird! It's a brain! It's bird brain! Feelings—master them! Instincts—rehabilitate them as higher consciousness! Dark recesses of the psyche—get the agents of the will to wire them! Your miserable self—a means to a better social and biological specimen. *Der Trotzkistische Übermunchkin*, the final product of the Subrealist International.

---

47. Ibid.
48. Ibid.
49. Ibid.

Socialism: Dystopian and Surrealistic

Trotsky was a leading advocate of Demonicratic Centralism. He said: "if the Party adopts a decision which one or other of us thinks unjust, he will say, just or unjust, it is my party, and I shall support the consequences of the decision to the end."[50] This is the political death drive in action, the most obsessive fixation on one particular expression of the Reality Principle that surrealism so diligently undermines, the ultimate expression of the Realpolitik that Surrealpolitik faithfully combats. Of course, even Trotsky could not live up to the exalted principles of Demonicratic Centralism, or else his own end would have taken place shortly after a show trial in which he confessed his sins and commended Comrade Stalin on finally achieving the noble goal of Socialism in One Country.

If the mystifying appeal of Trotsky in some surrealist circles seems like a form of mass hysteria of the other than fun kind, the attraction of Marx to surrealists is quite easy to understand. Marx was one of the greatest dialectical thinkers and was a master ironist. And surrealism is the moment to moment practice of dialectic and ironism in thought and action. The affinity with Marx is self-evident. Löwy cites Breton in the *Second Manifesto* as saying that "the Hegelian-Marxist dialectic is at the heart of the philosophy of Surrealism."[51] One could even turn the tables and say that the *surrealism* is at the *heart* of the Hegelian-Marxist dialectic. It is the heart of a heartless dialectic. At its worst, Hegelian-Marxist or any dialectic deteriorates into a mechanized, preconceived view of where things are going. At its best, it is wild at heart. It expresses the crazy anti-logic of unexpected reversals and shocking emergences, of the discovery of objectivity at the core of the subject, and of subjectivity at the heart of things. It abjures any neat synthesis or any privileged *telos*. And Marx is underneath it all a great romantic. Hegel may have said that all we need is R-E-S-P-E-C-T, but Marx said that "All we need is Love." "The greatest wealth" for the human being is "the other human being!"[52]

---

50. Speech at 13th Party Congress (May, 1924), quoted at http://www.marxists.org/history/etol/writers/souvar/works/stalin/ch08.htm.

51. Löwy, p. 3.

52. "Private Property and Communism," at http://www.marxists.org/archive/marx/works/1844/manuscripts/comm.htm. Actually, the young Hegel came under the spell of the Age of Aquarius perhaps even more than the young Marx. See "The Spirit of Christianity and Its Fate," and "Love" in the *Early Theological Writings*.

Marx once said "I am not a Marxist."[53] He also pointed out that if we are not complete idiots, "our opinion of an individual is not based on what he thinks of himself."[54] And as anybody familiar with dialectic knows, things always both are what they are not, and are not what they are. But just remember, this is not some sloppy "anything goes" procedure: they *are* and *are not* in a determinate, though perhaps very strange, way, so it's best to check. And if you check out Marx, or the various Marx's, you will find that the dialectical one, or ones, often go in a rather surrealistic and even anarchic direction. "Tendance Groucho" took a while to mature, or perhaps demature, but it's been around for a long time.

And Now, a Word from the Text

To return to Löwy's book—a strong point in it is his effort to retrieve the memory of several extraordinary but forgotten moments and figures in the history of surrealism. An example is his chapter on Claude Cahun, "non-Jewish Jewess, androgynous woman, dissident Marxist, lesbian Surrealist" who said "my religion is paganism, including inspired figures such as Socrates, Buddha, and Kropotkin; and my (dialectical) method of thinking is taken from Heraclitus, Hegel, and Marx."[55] It's hard to imagine a more inspiring and challenging collection of influences. What's more, Cahun was capable of moving from poetic subversion to anti-Fascist resistance. She was sentenced by the Nazis to be decapitated, and at the last moment saved miraculously (unexpectedly? marvelously? dialectically?) by what else but "The Liberation." Cahun's story hints at the wealth of surrealist history that Löwy touches on, but one must look to other more comprehensive works to see them explored adequately.

Here are four brief passages randomly selected from the *Morning Star* through the method (that some will find familiar) of opening to random pages and pointing to a line, giving the book a chance to more or less speak for itself:

> *Surrealists define revolution . . . as an interruption of*
> *the monotonous rotation of Western civilization around*

---

53. For example, as quoted by Engels in a letter of 1890. See http://www.marxists.org/archive/marx/works/1890/letters/90_08_05.htm.

54. "Preface" to *A Contribution to the Critique of Political Economy*.

55. Löwy, pp. 65, 79.

*itself, to do away with this self-absorbed axis once and for
all and to open the possibilities for another movement:
the free and harmonic movement of a civilization of
passionate attraction. . . . If one could use one word
to describe [Vincent Bounoure's] personality, it would
be 'poetry' . . . In April 1925 Naville wrote a short
declaration. Originally intended for internal debate, it
was published the next year as a pamphlet including texts
by Antoinin Artaud, Michel Leiris, and André Masson. .
. . Of unprecedented scope, [the Chicago World Surrealist
Exhibition] featured more than six hundred works—
paintings, drawings, collages, photographs, assemblages,
games, sculptures, and objects—by well over a hundred
active surrealists from thirty-one countries.*[56]

Let's hope that book told you some useful things about itself. One
thing that it tells me is that although Löwy presents some helpful
information about surrealism and some useful insights into it, he doesn't
allow the surrealists' surrealism to speak for *itself* quite enough. On the
other hand, he offers an introductory guide to the fascinating political
dimensions of surrealism, and the book will be most successful if it
leads the reader into the vast, astonishing literature of surrealism itself.
Fortunately, there are several works that put the reader on the fast track
to surreality and surrealpolitik.

Through the Retina of Actual Imaginary Experiences

Penelope Rosemont's *Surrealist Women* is a 500-page "international
anthology" that is required reading for anyone interested in the
surrealist movement and its history, including the diverse directions that
surrealpolitik has taken. About one-hundred women are represented,
including well-know figures such as Leonora Carrington, Nancy Cunard,
Frida Kahlo, Jacqueline Lamba, Mary Low, Joyce Mansour, Nadja, and
Meret Oppenheim, and many others who should be known by any
lover of surreality, creative anarchy and the wild imagination. The work
includes a wealth of material on surrealist politics. It explores topics such
as revolution, war and peace, working class struggle, oppression and
liberation—including its racial, sexual, and political dimensions.

In his perceptive introduction to *Morning Star*, Donald LaCoss

56. Ibid., pp. 6, 87, 45,111.

calls the May '68 General Strike in Paris "the best political fit" for the political dimension of surrealism "in more than forty years."[57] He notes the failure of Löwy to address this in the book. LaCoss was being rather indulgent in merely noting that the author "stops short,"[58] for what he is really pointing out is that Löwy conspicuously avoids, or perhaps represses, a rather momentous topic that relates to the deepest dimensions of surrealist politics. Not only did May '68 help bring out the anarchistic implications of surrealist and situationist politics, it also helped bring out the more surrealist and situationist dimensions of anarchism, and purge it of some of its more rigid, regressive and ideological vestiges. Anyone interested in exploring the implications of surrealist politics cannot afford to neglect its relationship to the whole soixante-huitard culture that emerged, its possibilities and limitations, its relation to reality, unreality, desire, imagination, surreality, and subreality. And this is exactly the sort of project that Rosemont takes on repeatedly in *Surrealist Women*. For example, it includes a section of almost one-hundred pages (nearly the length of Löwy's whole book) on "The Making of 'May '68' and Its Sequels"[59] in which the libertarian, anti-authoritarian, anarchistic dimensions of the events and their influence are recognized.

Though Rosemont's book is on surrealist women, she takes time to defend what she sees as the generally anti-patriarchal sensibilities of surrealist men. She says that not only did they "reject such 'masculine prerogatives' as law and order, reason and logic, they went so far as to champion their opposites, the so-called feminine virtues (or vices): intuition, impulsiveness, and 'passivity' (as in automatic writing and trance-speaking)."[60] However, she also points out that surrealist women have in many ways gone far beyond the men: "in surrealism, the adjective *wild* has always been a term of the highest prestige. But it is primarily the women in surrealism who stressed these matters."[61] This proclivity for wildness has perhaps been one reason why surrealist women have been less subject to the pitfalls of many male surrealists —a lack of appreciation of wild nature, an attraction to political sectarianism, an inability to overcome some sexist attitudes, a certain rigidity of character.

57. Löwy, p. xxix.
58. Ibid.
59. *Surrealist Women*, pp. 283-379.
60. Ibid, p. xlv,
61. Ibid., p. li.

Rosemont says that "surrealism's sense of freedom—its undeviating, irreducible, physical insistence on freedom—continues to distinguish it from all the other political and intellectual currents of our time."[62] This also distinguishes it, though it never entirely separates it, from much of the anarchist tradition (in fact, the part that has become most canonical, especially academically). The surrealist sense of freedom has been deeper and more experiential than that of most forms of anarchism. When it has intersected with anarchism, surrealism has helped infuse it with the substance and the spirit of freedom and countered the tendency, typical of political movements and ideologies, to get lost in the form and the letter. Surrealism helps make anarchism less *ismic* and more *anarchic*.

Rosemont goes a long way in demonstrating how it does this. Here's a random sampling of passages that hint at the imaginary force of the selections included in *Surrealist Women*:

> *I was transforming my blood into comprehensive energy— masculine and feminine, microcosmic and macrocosmic— and also into a wine which was drunk by the moon and the sun. . . . And there appeared to me a woman with chains upon her wrists, riding on a bicycle; and in her hand a banner bearing these words: THERE ARE NO MORE WHORES IN BABYLON. . . . Without beginning or end, memories and their ectoplasm, photographs come to contradict themselves on the retina of actual imaginary experiences. . . . I have thrust my knife through her pretty shirt, her hands are white and cold under the sheets. Mine are too much alive; they have no strength. But in her palm I see a tiny fruit, studded with pink tiny fragments which I melt between my fingers.[63]*

Exterminating the Blind Flags

Franklin Rosemont's foreword to Ron Sakolsky's important work *Surrealist Subversions* begins with a quote from Breton: "An anarchist world and a surrealist world: They are the same."[64] The realm of surreality is the world that appears beyond all archés and all archisms,

---

62. Ibid., p. 391.
63. Ibid., pp. 151, 89, 326, 220.
64. *Surrealist Subversions*, p. 15.

beyond the limits of domination. This impressive collection consists of seven hundred pages of evidence of these anarchistic dimensions of surrealpolitik.

Rosemont goes on to say that the basic aim of surrealism is "to realize poetry in everyday life."[65] Poesis signifies creation, creativity, and the creative spirit. Poesis is everywhere around us and everywhere within us and everywhere in between. It is true that in an important sense "realizing" poetry means the greater *actualization* of this poesis. But in another significant sense it means the *coming to awareness* of this all-pervasive creativity. It's like the Buddha-nature in Zen. Realizing the Buddha-nature means achieving awakened mind through realizing that it has always been present (though often in an absent sort of way, of course). Similarly, realizing poetry means recognizing poetry as *the real real* (in reality, *the real reals*), so that the impoverished, fetishized, objectified image of the real is displaced by the overabundant,

Clarence Laughlin, détournement by Stephen Duplantier

Masked Mardi Gras revelers post-parade with added head of a fly.

---

65. Ibid., p. 27.

limitless, infinitely-dimensional realms of surreality. Poetic realization is this anarchic, derealizing, transrealizing, surrealization. It means surrendering our selves to the Reality Non-Principle. We discover that there is no One and no one. We can relax and enjoy the multiplicity. *Surrealist Subversions* introduces the reader to the vast multiplicity within surrealism itself, and focuses heavily on the diverse dimensions of surrealist politics. It includes entire sections on revolution, capitalism, patriarchy, sexual repression, racism, authoritarian religion, ecodefense, and working class organization. Many of these themes run through the rest of this huge collection. And it doesn't just give the usual lip-service to anti-patriarchy and concede token representation to women. It includes about seventy-five articles, in addition to many works of art, by women. Finally, it's a volume thick with surrealpolitik, a basic guide book into the world of surrealist politics. One can easily gather this from the following random passages:

> POETRY (as opposed to literature): breathing like a
> machinegun, exterminating the blind flags of immediate
> reality . . . . Desire, sexuality, and its relationship to
> revolt have always been central themes in the music,
> but too often avoided by well-meaning defenders of
> the race concerned about reinforcing stereotypes of
> Black promiscuity. . . . Back in Southern California in
> the world of esoteric-occultist printers and bookmen,
> Jaque's thoughts on society, health, spirituality, and
> ethics matured as he studied theosophy, Buddhism, zen,
> semantics, and ebonite Christianity. . . . The best work
> understands that sexual identities and practices are
> lived through race and class and can only be understood
> historically.[66]

Thing of the Future

A number of years ago I was part of a group that picketed regularly outside the headquarters of neo-Fascist politician David Duke, who was at the time waging a frighteningly strong campaign for governor of Louisiana. Duke's henchmen loved to taunt the left-wing protesters.

---

66. Ibid., pp. 158, 139, 688, 305.

"...exterminating the blind flags of immediate reality..."

thing of the past!" One of our picketers responded immediately, "And anarchism is a thing of the future."[67]

What might be added to this truth is that communism, not in its degraded, state-capitalist and bureaucratic centralist sense, but in its

---

67. New Orleans poet Dennis Formento deserves credit for this spontaneous retort which mystified the obnoxious Fascist, who, thankfully, was reduced to silence at least for the moment.

most primordial Pre-Ancientist sense of the free commons, is also a thing of the future. And as one can begin to gather from Löwy's account and can see quite vividly from the Rosemonts' and Sakolsky's works, surrealism (including the surrealpolitik that goes along with it) is a thing with many futures. Many anarchic futures.

"...the impoverished, fetishized, objectified image of the real is displaced by the overabundant, limitless, infinitely-dimensional realms of surreality."

Sors Piorum ("The Fate of the Pious") by Johann Theodor de Bry, from *Proscenium vitæ humanæ siue Emblematum Secvlarium, Iucundissima, & artificiosissima varietate Vitæ Humanæ & seculi huius deprauati mores, ac studia peruersissima.* Frankfurt 1627. Herzog August Digital Library, Wolfenbüttel.

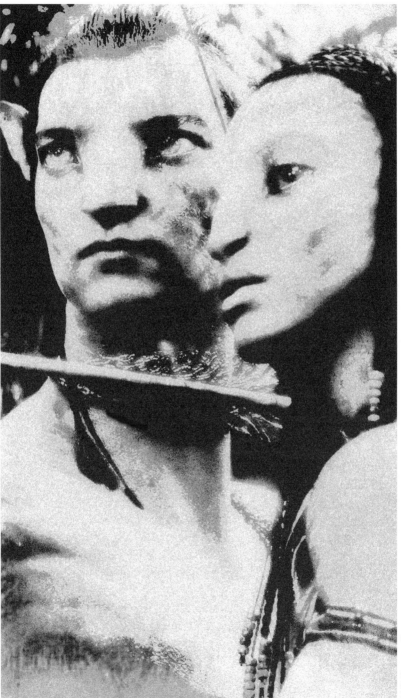

20th Century Fox

4

INTERGALACTIC BLUES:
FANTASY AND IDEOLOGY IN
AVATAR

The Secret of *Avatar*

*A*vatar is the highest-grossing film of all time—in the U.S., in at least thirty-one other countries, worldwide, and, as far as we know, in the entire universe. Its huge production and promotional cost of nearly $500 million is dwarfed by gross receipts of nearly $3 billion. This exceeds the GNP of at least 77 countries. Let's face it. It's the most important film in history. However, this is not because of the money it's raked in. A number of cinematic nullities have pulled in a huge gross. It's not because of the plot, the acting, or the directing. All of these are miserable failures. And it's certainly not because of the supposedly progressive and ecologically enlightened message. That's all a complete fake.

Avatar is the most important film in history in one very precise sense. *No film has ever revealed in such a spectacular way the functioning of ideology in cinema.* *Avatar* is unsurpassed in the history of cinema in showing the ways in which ideology turns things into their precise opposite. Perhaps most important, it reveals with complete clarity the fact that no message, no matter how formally radical or revolutionary it might be, will have any salutary effect on the real world, if that message is transmitted through the dominant media. It reveals the ultimate truth of mass media and of the cinematic spectacle. It reveals exactly what it means to be a spectator in mediatized society.

One of the primary rules of ideology critique is always to look for the purloined letter. Yes, "the truth is out there." And usually not that far out there. It pops up several times in relation to *Avatar*. For example, the director, James Cameron, slips up and explains exactly what his film is about, in completely non-ideological terms, in an interview shortly before it was released. He says, "We're telling the story of what happens when a technologically superior culture comes into a place with a technologically inferior indigenous culture and there are resources there that they want . . . . It never ends well."[1]

I suppose that it's not entirely astounding that the writer and director of a film might on some level actually know what his own film is really about. The astonishing thing is that almost everyone who sees the film thinks it's about exactly the opposite, and he does his best to make them think this. They think it's the story of how a very cool indigenous culture kicks the ass of a very nasty technologically advanced Empire, while a young American wins the very tall Blue Girl of his dreams. They think it's a story that ends *really well*. Unlike these viewers, Cameron seems, at least for a moment, to recognize the difference between the "real story" of *Avatar* and the superficially impressive but inanely idiotic supplementary narrative that pretends to subvert the real one, while in fact powerfully reinforcing it.

It's Really Special

We will take a very detailed look at the *real story* of *Avatar*. But first, let's consider the film's vaunted technical achievements and what we might call the "manifest story," that is, what almost everybody seems to think it's about: the plot. First, those really special effects. As one reviewer quipped, *Avatar*'s 3-D technology puts it "light-years ahead" of other films. Actually, *Avatar* is not only a considerable *cosmological distance* ahead of the others but even a whole *ontological dimension* ahead of the pack, since it appeared in some theaters in 4-D. The fourth dimension consists of elements that not only *seem* to be outside the

1. http://www.telegraph.co.uk/culture/film/6720156/James-Cameron-interview-for-Avatar.html.

screen, but *really are* outside it. Credit is usually given to John Waters for introducing 4-D with "Odorama" but this was only a new version of "Smell-O-Vision," which goes all the way back to 1960, the beginning of this cinematic New Frontier. The *idea* of the Fourth Dimension can be found at least as early as Buster Keaton's masterpiece, "Sherlock, Jr." (1924), in which Buster is depicted as going back and forth through a movie screen.

When *Avatar* first introduced 4-D in Korea, no Na'vi managed to fly their pterodactyloid aircraft through the movie screen into the theater, but dimension-bending techniques included moving seats, the smell of explosives, sprinkling water, wind, laser lights, plus twenty-five other special effects.[2] The cinematic world historical significance of 4-D is that it moves the techniques of imagineering beyond the limits of the screen into the more immediate environment of the viewers. It's a step in the direction of the totalizing of the imaginary experience, an increasing colonization or occupation of imaginary distance, the gap of fantasy. This could, on the one hand, work to subvert the powers of illusion, to the extent that ambient control distracts from the intensity of focus on the screen, the primary matrix of imaginary power. On the other hand, to the extent that it successfully reinforces the fantasy, it expands the empire of illusion, projecting it spatially outward toward the subject.

The ultimate *telos* of this movement from screen to subject will ironically result in a complete collapse of the process and effect a suspension of the distance traversed. In the end, images will be generated directly in the brains of what was once quaintly called "the viewers," or "the audience," in reference to the then obsolete forms of sensory transmission. In a sense, the audience will become on a certain level (What should we say, "a fleet"? No, that's not quite right. Let's say "a multitude.") *a multitude of drones.* Or, to put it in a more mystified and mythologized form, they will become *a multitude of avatars.*

Dreaming the Impossible Dream

In contrast to the futuristic nature of its special effects, *Avatar* is much more presentist, and, even backward-looking and traditionalist, in the conceptualization and realization of its central narrative. The film begins with stereotypically "primitive" music and scenes of the primal forest.

2. http://www.independent.co.uk/arts-entertainment/films/news/
lsquoavatarrsquo-in-4d-at-korean-theaters-1905267.html.

We're thrown immediately in the world of romantic exoticism, soon to be contrasted with a dismal world of technological domination. We're transported 150 years in the future, long after Corporate Capitalism and the State have ravaged Planet Earth. We have entered the era in which corporations not only rule the world, or what's left of it, but are well on the way to ruling the universe. The story takes place in one particular corner of the universe, the moon Pandora, where the RDA Corporation has moved in to exploit a mineral of almost inestimable value called "Unobtainium." As Selfridge, the top corporate manager on Pandora says, "Their damn village is sitting right over the richest unobtanium deposit for a hundred klicks in any direction." The corporate rulers are not only dreaming the impossible dream, they are in the process of obtaining the unobtainable resource that will allow them to reap previously unreapable profits. And they don't have to go a single additional klick to do it.

While corporations have thoroughly trashed the earth, they seem to have survived global collapse in some unexplained manner, only to move on to new commanding heights. In the process, they have realized the hopes of Milton Friedman and the anarcho-capitalists and replaced national armies with powerful Private Defense Forces. We get to see what the State looks like when it's fully privatized, rather than being negated and abolished. RDA's Free Enterprise Army is ready, willing, and—let's face it—more than able to move in and overwhelm any resistance from the natives. We know what time it is. It's turkey-shoot time.

Next, we meet the Blue Turkeys. The natives are a tribal society consisting of Humanoids of Color called "the Na'vi." They are blue-skinned (a shade called "Na'vi Blue," we assume), ten feet tall, highly intelligent and physically powerful. They have a traditionalist, nature-worshiping, communal society that lives in complete balance with nature. They practice an animistic and pantheistic religion that centers around the worship of a great Mother Goddess, Eywa. Their planet, we are told, is a kind of Giant Brain in which there is "some kind of electrochemical communication between the roots of the trees." It is "a global network" with "more connections than the human brain." This is "All My Relations" updated. While real indigenous people have thought in terms of relationships of kinship and cycles of gift exchange, in *Avatar* the ultimate relations become technological and cybernetic ones, albeit in a primitivistically mystified form.

Signifying Monkeys

Unfortunately for the invading forces of free enterprise, Pandora is completely inhospitable to humans. Not only is it populated by hordes of ferocious creatures intent on killing and eating folks, the atmosphere is completely lethal to Homo sapiens. The Corporation's primary solution to this problem is to engineer avatars, hybrid creatures containing a blend of Na'vi and human DNA. This allows the nervous systems of the human and his or her corresponding avatar to be "in tune." Though the avatar appears to be a normal Na'vi, it can be remote-controlled by the human who shares its DNA.

The protagonist, Jake Sully, has come to Pandora to take over his murdered twin brother's avatar (since only someone with identical DNA can do this.). Jake is a former Marine who lost use of his legs in military action. His superior, Dr. Grace Augustine, has little confidence in him and consigns him, or on the physical level, his avatar, to guard duty. So it's time to hook him up to his avatar. As soon as this is done, Jake immediate freaks out, crashing into everything in the lab before escaping and going temporarily AWOL as he cavorts through the Pandoran countryside. There is a ridiculous gap between the real Jake's personality and that of his avatar. Jake is chastened by tragedy and to a certain degree reflective. His avatar turns out to be a charmingly stupid, somewhat gonzoid cartoon hero. This might seem strange, since nothing about either the human genes or the Na'vi ones would fully explain this. However, it soon becomes evident that all the Na'vi characters have a good dose of Disney DNA also, and these genes seem to be particularly dominant in the avatar called "Jakesully."

After calming down, Jake's avatar joins a mission in the Pandoran forest. He gets separated from the others and is nearly devoured immediately by the terrifying local fauna, before being miraculously saved by the Na'vi princess Neytiri, who happens to be in the neighborhood and wipes out the scary creatures. Despite all the technological sophistication of the Corporation, Jake seems to have almost no training for survival on Pandora. It's amazing that he lasted even long enough for the Magic Princess to save him. Neytiri notices immediately how difficult it is to convey anything about Pandora to thickheaded Sky People like Jake. Mo'at, the female shaman, agrees. Showing the trans-planetary nature of clichés, she remarks, "It is hard to fill a cup which is already full." However, this lovable idiot begins to grow on Neytiri. She takes him to the communal dwelling place, an enormous thousand-foot high tree, which is appropriately called "Home Tree." Despite widespread suspicion about the aliens and their avatars, the Na'vi decide to allow Jake to stay and to teach him about the culture.

At this point in the story, we come to one of the things the audience would be most curious about: What is a Na'vi drug trip like? As part of his education, Jake's avatar gets to have a vision. Mo'at purifies his body with holy smoke, and then takes "a glowing purple WORM" from some rotten old wood and deposits it in Jake's mouth for him to chew. Immediately, those around him "seem to TRANSFORM, becoming threatening," and "SPACE is utterly distorted, and SOUND as well—echoing, THUNDEROUS." He sees "a ring of glowing trees, which seem miles high," and everything is "bathed in spectral radiance." There's more, but you get the point. It all ends with a vision of "a diving LEONOPTERYX," a huge ferocious creature, bearing down on him. However, you have to check the script to find all this out, because the audience gets to see none of it. Apparently, it was judged to be too dangerous. In fact, the whole movie is about, and in a sense is, a drug experience. It's all about escapism through spacing out, but none of this can be expressed too explicitly. So the audience is robbed of this particular cheap thrill. We move on.

Winning (Or Else Wasting) Hearts and Minds

Meanwhile, back at the space colony, Jake catches up on the Corporation's strategy on Pandora. As he summarizes it: "That's how it's done. When people are sitting on shit you want, you make them your enemy. Then you're justified in taking it." However, the Corporation and its army, presumably after reading ancient military manuals from Vietnam and Afghanistan, has adopted the tactic of trying to "win the hearts and minds" of the natives before massacring them. However, to their surprise (no ancient history books having survived) this has been a complete failure and relations have deteriorated. So, while bribing the Na'vi into compliance would be the Corporation's preferred, most cost-effective tactic, the military is fully prepared to annihilate what they see as backward Blue Gooks, should this be necessary. As Selfridge puts it, "killing the indigenous looks bad, but there's one thing shareholders hate more than bad press—and that's a bad quarterly statement. Find me a carrot to get them to move, or it's going to have to be all stick."

Jake's avatar has been accepted into Na'vidom, so this infiltrating avatar is the last hope for arranging a non-genocidal, non-stick solution to the problem of getting the goods. Selfridge tells Jake what his mission is: "Look, Sully—find out what these blue monkeys want." Col. Miles Quaritch adds that Jake will "get his legs back," courtesy of the Corporation, if he succeeds in betraying his new Na'vi friends. We can feel at home in this future world. Big Brother still pours huge investments into top-priority military hardware, while at the same time strictly rationing non-essential medical treatment that could merely make someone's life worthwhile.

Jake continues his mission among the Na'vi, but is increasingly won over by the natives. They decide that his education has progressed to the point that he can be officially adopted into the tribe. Now a full-fledged Hometreeboy, he aids his newfound bluepeeps in resisting an attack by the Corporation's army. Beginning to emerge as a budding tribal hero, he single-handedly disables one of the Corporation's huge military vehicles. As a rookie tribesman, Jake gets the rather individualist, patriarchal right to choose a mate, but in an act of primitivistic political correctness, Jake and Neytiri end up choosing one another. Thus, they incidentally introduce romantic love into this communal tribal society, no doubt flouting tradition and the wisdom of the ancestors.

Monkey Business

Jakesully and Neytiri then consummate their union. The Na'vi may forgive the blue Romeo and Juliette for sacrilege or whatever, but it's hard to imagine that the audience will forgive the director for depriving them of the one thing they were most curious about: How do the Na'vi do it? Tragically, we get no idea what Blue Monkey Sex is really like. All we see is totally romanticized fore-foreplay and voilà, the lovers are peacefully intertwined, snoozing blissfully on the forest floor.

It goes quite otherwise in the unexpurgated script. Neytiri remarks, in a surprising move of tribal coquetterie, "Kissing is very good. But we have something better." Next, "she takes the end of her queue and raises it." Wanna queue? What do you think! "Jake does the same, with trembling anticipation. The tendrils at the ends move with a life of their own, straining to be joined." Ah, Ah! Autonomous part-objects! Extraterrestrial desiring machines! "MACRO SHOT—The tendrils INTERTWINE with gentle undulations." Ah! Ah! You earthlings

"Kissing is very good. But we have something better." Next, "she takes the end of her queue and raises it." Wanna queue?

20th Century Fox

can hardly imagine! "JAKE rocks with the direct contact between
his nervous system and hers." Total contact! The sexual body without
organs! "The ultimate intimacy." Ah! Ah! *Ahvatar!* Of course, "the
night" is itself "alive with pulsing energy as we DISSOLVE TO—LATER.
She is collapsed across his chest. Spent. He strokes her face tenderly."
Ah! Ah! Of course, we miss all of this, except a somewhat inexplicable
afterglow, in the film.

The closest we come to getting an answer in the film itself to "How do
the Na'vi do it?" is that they do it with their horses. Though the horses
are really more like flying prehistoric monsters. Neytiri introduces Jake
to "mounting" and "becoming one with" the creature. As the screenplay
relates the consummation of this extraordinary act of interspecies
intercourse:

> *JAKE nervously grips the surcingle of the mare. Neytiri holds
> its nose-ring while Jake clumsily mounts. Jake bends one of
> its ANTENNAE down to the tip of his queue. He hesitantly
> touches them together and— TIGHT SHOT— the tendrils
> INTERWEAVE. Jake's PUPILS DILATE and his mouth drops
> open. The horse's eyes also go wide and it HONKS nervously.
> Neytiri touches her fingertips to the neural interface." NEYTIRI
> says, "This is* shahaylu—*the bond. Feel her heartbeat, her breath.
> Feel her strong legs." Jake closes his eyes, nodding. One with the
> horse.[3]*

Is there any doubt about what's going on? Strangely, our director
seems to be afraid to depict Jake and Neytiri queuing, but he doesn't
hesitate to show Jake queuing his horse.

Meanwhile, back in civilization, Quaritch soon finds Jake's video
diary, in which that dumbass troop stupidly reveals all his traitorous
thoughts like some idiotic teenager putting videos of his drunken
malfeasances on YouTube. The Corporation decides to attack the Na'vi,
bomb HomeTree into oblivion, and grab the Unobtanium. Jake and Dr.
Grace are given an hour for a final attempt to reach an agreement with
the Na'vi, after which Shock and Awe will be unleashed. Jake and Grace's
plea for reasonable compromise with genocidal imperialism fails. When
their erstwhile tribal friends discover their role as emissaries for the

---

3. The text of the screenplay can be found at http://sashahalima.com/blog/2010/01/love-avatar-download-the-script-from-20th-century-fox/ and other sites.

Corporation, they accuse them of being spies (that is, precisely what they have been) and take them prisoner. The attack commences, fire and brimstone rain down, and in the holocaust HomeTree is immolated along with many of the Na'vi. Back at the military-industrial complex, Jake and Dr. Grace are disconnected from their captured avatars and thrown in the brig. One of their allies, a wise Latina, releases them, but Dr. Grace is seriously wounded during the escape. She later dies among the Na'vi.

In a major turning point in the narrative, Jake's avatar gets loose and proves himself by taming the Great Leonopteryx, alias Toruk, a monstrous flying creature that has only been subdued five time in the entire history of the Na'vi. Thus, Jake's avatar, the former bumbling blue idiot, becomes the Superhero of Na'vidom and the leader of hordes of warriors from other clans, who begin arriving in burgeoning numbers. The Corporation launches an overwhelming and seemingly irresistible attack, using all the firepower the martial imagination can muster. However, just as Shock and Awe seems on the verge of winning, Jake's avatar manages to blow up Quaritch's gigantic aircraft and rampaging hordes of giant prehistoricoid creatures stampede and decimate the advancing army. Victory is snatched from the jaws of defeat by the jaws of prehistoric monsters and by what looks pretty much like good old American Ingenuity and True Grit on the part of Jake's avatar. Quaritch survives the battle and almost ruins the fun by cutting off Jake's oxygen, but Neytiri saves the day by skewering the Colonel and rescuing Jake at the last possible moment. *Blugrrl power rules!*

The epic concludes with all but a few of the hopelessly unregenerate humans parading back to their spacecraft, defeated and dejected, ready to return to their ruined world (presumably until "Pandora Syndrome" wears off and they find another planet with Unobtainium, or maybe just Difficulttoobtainium, to plunder). The Na'vi perform a ritual in which Jake's spirit transmigrates completely into his now super-heroic avatar body. As we will see, this signifies that the Apotheosis of the Drone is complete.

Theory I: Like Wow!

But not everyone sees it this way. There have been a wide range of interpretations of *Avatar* that go in various directions, though most take it as a given that the central theme is the triumph of noble savagery and the beneficent forces of nature over a corrupt, greedy and generally iniquitous civilization. For example, Ido Hartogsohn in "*Avatar*: The Psychedelic Worldview and the 3-D Experience"[4] interprets *Avatar* as a kind of New Age Revelation. He says that,

> *it is as anti-civilizational and anti-technological as a John Zerzan book, psychedelic like a Terrence McKenna talk, and glorifies the indigenous and shamanic world view. The fact that some people have failed to appreciate these highly explicit traits in* Avatar, *and call it clichéd or hackneyed is, to my mind, largely based on blindness to* Avatar's *role as a mythic specimen of our culture.*

Terrance is long gone, but I'd like to check with John on this. But, OK, let's admit it. It's a mythic specimen of our culture. The question is: "A specimen of what?"

How neo-primitivist is it? Hartogsohn cites examples of plot elements that are taken from authentic tribal cultures and concludes that these show that "the *Avatar* story is as anti-civilizational and neo-primitivist as it gets." He admits that it is "a highly ambivalent and even paradoxical film. It uses the most advanced technology to go on a long harangue against technology. But it has the maybe naïve hope that our pod experience, like Jake's, will make us want to leave our pods and reconnect with our bodies." Yeah, sure. As they say, "hopefully…" But in reality there's little (read: no) chance that such a film can have that effect, especially since the solution to Jake's problem is not *reconnecting* with his own body, or coming to terms with its limitations, as actual living earthlings might have to do, but rather it is *casting it off* in favor of a technologically engineered one. Of course, if you believe in New Age magic merged with cybernetics, you can hope that the technobody will eventually morph into a real person rather than remaining a techno-nobody. But nobody in their right mind can really believe that.

It's not surprising that *Avatar* should go over well in Lalaland, since it's so full of New Age fakery. For example, Jake observes that the whole planet is a vast system of energy that the Na'vi can plug into—sometimes literally. It sounds really far out, like those holistic, personally empowering, non-polluting electric cars (all you do is plug them into the grid at night). "They see a network of energy that flows through all living things. They know that all energy is only borrowed." Yet there is no evidence that the Na'vi have to pay back all the energy they drain from

4. http://www.realitysandwich.com/avatar_psychedelic_worldview_3d.

the system. True, they die, but this just gives back a small amount of the total energy they use. Therefore, this is just ideology—they actually use a surplus of energy, draining it continually from the system, but they claim that they are only borrowing it and will pay it back. The Na'vi are not far from the kind of self-deception that is endemic in some Green and most New Age circles. The Na'vi are, in fact, a mythologized embodiment of precisely such false consciousness.

Hartogsohn, however, thinks that it is "no less than amazing" that such a revolutionary film, "with its psychedelic qualities and ideas, shamanic values, and indigenous politics," and which "challenges all that is sacred to western materialistic thought and champions shamanic ideas and values deemed to be ludicrous by the dominator culture" has "already earned more than a billion dollars and is quite probably on its way to becoming the highest grossing film of all time." Right. Show me the money. The New Age Revolution is over and the primitive has won, all on the basis of box-office receipts.

A hard act to follow, this powerful assault on Western civilization. What could possibly come next? Hartogsohn tells us exactly. After the Revolution comes the Renaissance. "Considering that the next big 3-D event is Tim Burton's *Alice in Wonderland*, a story jammed with weird acting mushrooms and even weirder realities, it seems that we might be facing a kind of psychedelic renaissance brought on by 3-D cinema." In other words, after a "fundamental challenge" to the "reigning values" of the "dominator culture," we don't do something mundane like starting an actual, real-world revolution to put the new values into effect. No, we move on to *Alice in Wonderland*.

Theory II: Objet Petit @

Please, let's move on. More interestingly, Layla AbdelRahim gives us the critical anarcho-primitivist interpretation of *Avatar*.[5] Like most commentators, she focuses primarily on the manifest content of the plot. In her view, "the film is primarily about the two clashing world-views at the core of the relationship between the civilized and the wild" and "Jake represents the conscience of the civilized awakened by his ability to finally learn." And, of course, this is exactly what we see in the surface narrative. It's a morality tale in which bad civilization is juxtaposed to

5. Layla AbdelRahim, "Avatar: An Anarcho-Primitivist Picture of the History of the World" at http://layla.miltsov.org/avatar-an-anarcho-primitivist-picture-of-the-history-of-the-world/.

good primitivism, with Jake as the mediating term. In a sense, he's like the Ursula LeGuin figures (in *The Dispossessed, Always Coming Home*, etc.) who are able to live in two worlds and reveal something about each that the inhabitants of each don't see.[6] However, in Jake's case, he doesn't *truly* mediate. In fact, there is never really any mediation possible between the corrupt, evil society and the good community. LeGuin's mediators really mediate between us, those capable of deliverance from the corrupt, evil world, and the imagined good society, which is really a representation of the liberatory moments of our own human history. Jake is utterly incapable of doing this, because of the fraudulent nature of the "good" alternative offered in *Avatar*.

In the end, the utter impossibility of his work of mediation is symbolized by the disappearance of his human body, his direct connection to one of his worlds. He's a partially vanishing mediator. Jake *qua* Jake disappears. There's just no hope for the human, all too human. Everything in the end is A (for Avatar) OK. But one must wonder whether the remaining human DNA in Jake's avatar would not come back to haunt the Na'vi. Of course, this is a sequel that will never be produced. We are to fantasize Jake's avatar as in the end a Na'vi "without remainder," though we know that there is, as always, a remainder. But AbdelRahim still entertains the possibility that Jake/avatar Jake could function as a successful mediating term.

To support the anarcho-primitivism thesis, AbdelRahim points out that Jake "does not come there as a leader, but as someone responsible for the disclosure of vital information about the enemy." There are several problems, though, with this claim. First, he comes as a spy, and secondly, he is fully ready to become a leader, and he in fact ends up doing so in a big way. He proves that a hybrid with just enough Gringo genes can do what none of the living Na'vi are capable of doing, for good or evil. AbdelRahim contends that the message of the film is that "if life is to survive against the machine, it is vital to respond as brutally as the invader attacks in order to stop the disease. Resistance is going to cost lives, but it is necessary, if one wants to save the balance of life." The problem is that if this is really the message of the film, it is a message that goes nowhere with the vast majority of the audience, and could hardly be expected to have any real effect. It's an undeliverable message, and what kind of message is that? It's at best a nominal message rather than a real one. And, in fact, it's the antithesis of the real one of the film.

6. For a brilliant discussion of the importance of outsiderism, see Andrei Codrescu, *The Disappearance of the Outside* (Addison-Wesley, 1990).

AbdelRahim ultimately recognizes this, and for this reason, her interpretation is far superior to most of the Romantic primitivist views of *Avatar*. In the end, she fully acknowledges fatal "problems with this anarcho-primitivist work of art." She might have said that the big one is that it's neither "anarcho-primitivist" nor a "work of art." Instead, she notes that "it is based on the symbolic representation relying on the use of the same materials that are at the basis of our alienation from the world," and that the medium assumes "the overt acknowledgment of the 'fakeness' of the experience," and thus cannot "convince us of truth." She points out that "Cameron uses the same machines, technologies and money that devastate the wilderness he tells us we need to save," and that what the audience comes for is not revolutionary propaganda, but "entertainment and a 3-dimensional experience of violence and sci-fi." So, we might add that far from "convincing us of truth," *Avatar* indeed *perpetuates lies.* The lies are embedded in the structure of the corporate capitalist film industry, in the cinematic process, and, far more than AbdelRahim concedes, even in the dramatic structure of the film itself, as we shall see.

Theory III: What Do You Mean "We," Paleface?

Right-wing columnist David Brooks picks up on one of the central structural flaws of *Avatar* in his article "The Messiah Complex."[7] However, Brooks has to get this year's, if not this decade's, "Bad Faith in Film Criticism" award for writing the most blatantly hypocritical review of a film. According to Brooks, the great sin of *Avatar* is that it espouses what he calls the "White Messiah Fable." According to his account, the White Messiah Fable is "the oft-repeated story about a manly young adventurer who goes into the wilderness in search of thrills and profit. But, once there, he meets the native people and finds that they are noble and spiritual and pure. And so he emerges as their Messiah, leading them on a righteous crusade against his own rotten civilization. Audiences like it because it is so environmentally sensitive. Academy Award voters like it because it is so multiculturally aware. Critics like it because the formula inevitably involves the loincloth-clad good guys sticking it to the military-industrial complex." Brooks, as a good right-wing philistine, dislikes it for all the same reasons he thinks that the various idiots in the audience like it.

---

7. http://www.nytimes.com/2010/01/08/opinion/08brooks.html.

The irony of Brooks' criticism is that he attacks precisely the same evil ideology that he spends his entire life promoting. The problem he has with the film is that the White Messiah is named "Jake" and the pure people are called the "Na'vi." If the White Messiah were called "USA" or some representative thereof, and the saved were called "Iraq," "Afghanistan," or "Fillintheblankistan," there would be no problem. No one like Brooks is truly opposed to the White Messiah fable. It's just that believers don't call something "a fable" when it's in a form they believe in. What Brooks can't stand is seeing a perversion of the very mythology that is most dear to him. When he lists egregious examples of cinematic White Messiahism, he fails to register a single complaint against any Honky Hero who ventures out into the world of primitive barbarism to protect outposts of Western Civilization or to save the benighted primitive barbarians from themselves. It's only the Palefaced Paladins who defect to the enemy that get on Brooks's nerves. As late as 2008, Rambo could a still "venture into war-torn Burma, and rescue a group of Christian aid workers who were kidnapped by the ruthless local infantry unit"[8] carrying on the noble White Messianic tradition by personally killing 238 bad guys of color. But you won't hear a word of complaint from our Mr. Brooks.

Brooks' strategy requires him at once to vastly oversimplify the White Messiah theme and to exaggerate greatly its significance. The result necessitates a kind of pose of enlightened stupidity. His right-wing sensibilities are offended even by this vapid form of anti-imperialist nonsense, so he must attempt to justify his defensive reaction in the guise of anti-racism. However, this obliges him to get almost everything about the film wrong. For example, he thinks that its plot "rests on the stereotype that white people are rationalist and technocratic while colonial victims are spiritual and athletic." But this isn't true. The film depicts imperialists (not just "white people") as *extremely irrational* and technocratic, that is, more or less the way imperialists really are. He also claims that such a narrative "creates a sort of two-edged cultural imperialism. Natives can either have their history shaped by cruel imperialists or benevolent ones, but either way, they are going to be supporting actors in our journey to self-admiration." This is also an opportunistic distortion. It's true that Cameron in some ways perpetuates a repugnant and ridiculous racist stereotype. But in the end, despite the exaggerated heroics of Jake's avatar, he does not single-

---

8.   Internet Movie Data Base.

handedly "shape the history" of the Na'vi. Their victory is determined also by the resistance of the Na'vi themselves and by the "revenge of nature"—the latter in ways that have nothing at all to do with anything Jake does. And finally, the problem isn't that the story is secretly all about "self-admiration." In reality, the viewer can wallow in admiration for the primitive, while at the same time indulging in quite a bit of civilizational self-hatred. The problem is that all of this wallowing and indulging are made quite safe and nonthreatening, and take place fully within the context of the most conformist advanced technological consumerism.

Theory IV: The Function of the Fantasm

Not surprisingly, the always-incisive Slavoj Žižek goes much further than most other reviewers in revealing what the film is really about. In "Return of the natives,"[9] Žižek confronts directly the big issue in the film—the dialectic of fantasy and reality, both within the film, and in the relation between world of the film and the larger world. Of course, he unveils the film's naïve fantasy strategy, but he warns that the point is not that we "should reject *Avatar* on behalf of a more 'authentic' acceptance of the real world." He explains that rather "if we really want to change or escape our social reality, the first thing to do is change our fantasies that make us fit this reality." Which is, in fact, exactly the issue. *Avatar* reinforces these fantasies just as it creates the illusion of undermining them. But Žižek takes this in another direction. He says that because Jake is unable to change his fantasies, "his subjective position is what Jacques Lacan, with regard to de Sade, called *le dupe de son fantasme*," that is, the dupe of his fantasy, the victim of his own imagination. So, Žižek concludes, "the end of the film should be read as the hero fully migrating from reality into the fantasy world."

This criticism has much validity, on a certain level. The brutal world of the Corporation is "the real" relative to the cartoonish fantasy world of the Na'vi. So Jake's migration is in a sense equivalent to a tactic of escaping from the real world by being fully incorporated into the physical, cultural and spiritual world of Sponge Bob or The Smurfs. However, the imperialist world is, on several levels, a fantasy world also, so in a sense Jake migrates from a "real" fantasy world (one closer to the dominant fantasy) to a more fantastic, higher-order fantasy world. In

9. http://www.newstatesman.com/print/201003040015.

fact, we could interpret the whole plot after the opening scene as Jake's fantasy of overcoming his handicapped body and escaping from the world that caused his disaster. We can see one tragic narrative strand in *Avatar* as the story of a damaged subject who wants to secede from the hegemonic culture that mutilated him, but who doesn't know how to do so in any realistic way, and who thus seeks refuge in a ridiculous fantasy. If we follow this course of reasoning, we might say that Jake, fictional though he may be, can only achieve his goal vicariously, through us. Through our own temporary insanity of successful identification with a ridiculous cartoon, we allow the non-existent Jake to solve his existential problem.

The Big Monkey Does Not Exist

On the other hand, we can also see *Avatar* as the representation of the collective fantasy of the audience who find their world to be actually turning into the dystopian planet earth of the film. Žižek suggests that we might "imagine a sequel to *Avatar* in which, after a couple of years (or, rather, months) of bliss, the hero starts to feel a weird discontent and to miss the corrupted human universe." As I suggested earlier, something like this might be the kind of thing that would happen when Jakesully's human DNA kicks in. This is exactly what happens in the classic case of the brilliant ending of *Blue Velvet*, in which just as the triumphant protagonist Jeffrey begins to sit back and enjoy the American Dream, the creepy unreality of the putatively real world emerges. There is a return of the sublimely menacing repressed underside of that truly nightmarish world that masquerades as everyday ordinary reality. Using the imagery of the film, we might say that "the poison is in him"—the poison of the real and the poison of a subversive imaginary, represented by the hauntingly attractive character, Dorothy Vallens.

Avatar's audience must experience something like this on an unconscious level to the degree that they are not complete idiots and recognize the world of the Na'vi as fake and contrived. The Big Blue Monkey does not exist. As Jake says, fatefully, at the beginning of *Avatar*, in a powerful immanent critique of the film's entire flimsy fantasy structure, "sooner or later though, you always have to wake up." The problem is that *Avatar* allows the audience members to wake up from the dream into the nightmare, but far from helping them wake up from the nightmare, it actually prevents them from doing so. They must on some level of consciousness know that as the sullen earthlings file back on to their spacecraft for the trip back to a devastated McEarth, that this is really the audience filing out of the movie theater into the real world of late capitalism.

Žižek also calls Cameron on his rather brain-dead adherence to "the Hollywood formula for producing a couple," which he pushes to the point of "staging great historical events as the background to the formation of a couple" (for which he takes *Reds*, rightly, as the ultimate *reductio ad absurdum*). Like Brooks, though from a politically and philosophically opposite perspective, he stresses the centrality of the White Messiah theme. He points out that the plot gives the indigenous people no choice other than "either to be the victim of imperialist reality, or to play their allotted role in the white man's fantasy." Which is, as in the case of Brooks's reactionary interpretation, partially true, but not entirely adequate. To the extent that the narrative is seen as Jake's escape from the impasse of his disability through an elaborate fantasy, everything about the Na'vi, the Corporation and the epochal battle between good and evil merely plays a role in his fantasy.

However, the dialectic of the imaginary is more complex than this. On another level, Jake is captured by the fantasy-world of the Na'vi, and transformed by them, even to the point of fully becoming (even if not, of course, "fully becoming") a Na'vi. Furthermore, there is a moment in which Jake's heroic role results from his negation of his "whiteness" and his allowing the tribe and the forces of nature to work through him. This is the moment that allows many viewers to be taken in by the primitivism and anti-civilizationism of the film. The problem is not that this moment does not exist, that it's "White Messiah" all the way down, but that this moment is in the end a complete failure aesthetically, dramatically, psychologically, morally and politically. The problem is that the audience is ultimately "the victim of imperialist reality," and its fantasy can be trusted "to play its allotted role" in legitimating that reality, and in helping that reality adapt itself successfully to a new world of environmental concern and cultural sensitivity. This shows the degree to which Marcuse's concept of "repressive desublimation" in late capitalism still has validity. *Avatar* is the most advanced expression of the project called "commodify your dissent."

Doing Without Doing

What would "*Avatar* activism," mean, if the film were really capable of being a catalyst for such a thing? There is no lack of opportunities for it, and they are not thousands of klicks away, but well within the boundaries of the Milky Way. To take one example, for forty years the tribal people of West Papua have been fighting against ecological devastation and cultural genocide by the Freeport McMoRan Corporation and its ally the Indonesian state. And, as Žižek mentions, the Naxalite rebellion, which consists in large part of the resistance of indigenous people to exploitation by mining companies, was spreading through the forests of India just as *Avatar* was racking up three billion dollars in receipts by exploiting the theme of indigenous resistance as its central plot element (mining it for all it's worth, we might say). How many *Avatar* viewers have been inspired to come to aid of the Papuans? How many have gone to fight in the forest with the Naxalites? Has the film been a major motivation for even a single person to do anything like this? This is highly unlikely, for it is effective only in offering an imaginary substitute for any such action. The fantasies that it generates offer the audience opportunities for consumption of profit-generating, post-modernist, pseudo-subversive images. It remains light-years away from inspiring the production of any disruptive, so-19th-Century revolutionary acts.

Žižek points out the fateful problem of being *unable* to change ones fantasy. And there is, indeed, a tenacity and incorrigibility of the fundamental fantasy or, more accurately, the constellation of related fantasies that constitutes the dominant imaginary. The consequences of this incapacity are, as he indicates, often disastrous. But one of the most striking things about our late capitalist consumer culture is the range of opportunities that it offers to consumers and spectators precisely to *change* their fantasies in certain ways. While being entranced by the 3-D and 4-D special effects, and awed by the power of CGI, the audience can enter superficially and momentarily into an anarcho-primitivist fantasy, yet at the same time it will have no difficulty holding on to its technological utopian dream-world and other basic fantasies that are evoked, reinforced and gratified in a multitude of ways in everyday life. The primitivist fantasy, though it may be evoked again periodically, is incapable of challenging even minimally the normal productionist and consumptionist fantasies, the fantasies of the machine and the spectacle, that dominate ordinary experience. Any intense gratification of the primitivist fantasy will, of course, have residual effects. These can be expressed in activities such as recycling, buying green products, and viewing sequels to *Avatar*. And, in fact, there is an *Avatar* web site designed precisely to satisfy the urge to engage in such activities.

Avatars for Social Responsibility! Pandorans Without Borders!

One cannot claim that no social or ecological action has resulted from the film. If one goes to the *Avatar* web site, one will discover that Cameron has set up an activist project called "The Home Tree Initiative," with the professed goal of helping to save Homeplanet.[10] Contrary to the name, it's not an effort to create primitivist ecological communities inspired by the "Home Tree" of the Na'vi, much less any initiatives in eco-defense modeled after their resistance to the Intergalactic Capitalist Conspiracy. In reality, the initiative is just another tree-planting project. The two most non-transformative, non-threatening and eminently doable eco-gestures are recycling and tree planting, and since the movie features forests rather than sanitary landfills, the choice was obvious. As Cameron and producer Jon Landau tell us in a video on the website, they set a goal of planting one million trees in 2010. As they explain, "the time has come to stand up and be warriors for the earth." As it turns out, you can become an eco-warrior and fight the good, green fight without going through all the trouble of actually standing up.

One might quite reasonably wonder how planting trees qualifies one to be "a warrior for the earth." But this would miss the point. The "Home Tree Initiative" doesn't actually require the brave eco-warriors to plant even a single tree. In fact, they don't even have to contribute a single cent for anyone else to plant one. We are told that "20th Century Fox has partnered with The Earth Day Network to plant 1 million trees." Such major actors, along with cooperating nation-states, will take care of the planting. At ease, eco-troops. All you have to do is enlist for a little basic training of the imagination. The Path of the Eco-Warrior consists merely in signing up to "adopt a tree." That's it. You just *imagine* that

---

10.   http://www.avatarmovie.com/hometree/.

it's adopted and voilà, you're on the warpath. The idea is that a million eco-warriors willing to endure the perils of imaginary tree adoption will be recruited. Just consider what a million people who imagine that they have adopted a tree are capable of doing. Or not actually doing. Unfortunately, in spite of such less than heroic effort required to qualify as a "warrior for the earth," the Eco-Salvation Army remains badly understaffed. As of the end of the year, the web site stated that only 290,000 warriors/adoptive tree parents had reported for (non-)duty, while the other 710,000 remained AWOL. Perhaps the rest just imagined that they signed up.

For those *Avatar* fans who just aren't all that much into trees, the site offers more traditional online attractions. For example, if you're turned on by a different shade of green, you can enter the "Ultimate Avatar Sweepstakes" and win $50,000. Of course, I signed up immediately, hoping that I could be the kind of warrior who wins $50,000—by fighting against the odds, I suppose. I haven't won so far, but my new online friend, "Fox" urges me to continue to soldier on by "visiting www.avatarsweeps.com daily for more chances to win $50,000 and other instant-win prizes." Trying to be a good soldier and obey orders, I have continued to check the site. However, I've found that at a certain point you begin to feel less like an well-armed warrior and more like an unarmed target. For example, if you don't bother to uncheck a box, you are automatically "signed up to receive special announcements, updates and more from Twentieth Century Fox Home Entertainment." And you're told in the fine print that if you decide to adopt a tree (which will, of course, be planted whether you adopt it or not), you make an agreement to be bombarded with advertising for precisely the kind of consumerist junk that keeps the voracious ecocidal tree-eating Megamachine humming. And be warned: "By filling out and submitting this registration form I understand and agree that Twentieth Century Fox Home Entertainment may send me information about upcoming products, promotions and services and may use information about my activities on Fox web sites to determine what products, promotions and services are likely to be of interest to me." Until they can plant something directly in your brain that determines what your interests are, they need a little bit of cooperation on your part to effectively track and check up on you.

In addition, the website gives you the opportunity to play various eco-oriented games and get "badges." And best of all, you can actually "*become an Avatar*." I skipped the games, since I already had the thrill of winning badges long ago at summer camp, but never have I had the chance to become an actual avatar. I decided to become an avatar. Little did I suspect the mortal dangers of aspiring avatarhood. Two of my avatars were abruptly murdered somewhere in cyberspace because I had forgotten to "allow" the "popups" that are necessary for avatars fully to complete their gestation process. My abruptly aborted avatars even had pictures and their own personal Na'vi names before they were tragically short-circuited, shortly after the moment of cyber-conception. Let's hope that they are somewhere in avatar heaven with Eywa, or out happily planting trees in some deforested alternative universe. On the third try, I finally got my avatar, based on the "Cafardigras" 2006 Max Cafard Mardi Gras photo that I submitted.

The coincidence is amazing. My avatar is called Chok'tah. This name bears an uncanny similarity to the name of one of our local tribal groups, the Wild Chok'tah'toulas. Much as on Pandora, the tribal people here worship and dance around a Tree of Life. They even have a queen, called Sis'si Na'vi in one of the tribal dialects. And the nights are always alive with Spirits and Light. My avatar should feel right at home here. It's Pandora with Lagniappe. *Chok-tah-mo-fee-nah-nay!*

After all this harmless fun and consumerism, I was delighted to see that there was also a "take action now" link on the website. Finally, something for those who suspected that playing *Avatar*-related games or pretend-adopting a tree might not be the most effective means possible of fighting the Empire and saving Homeplanet. Finally, I would be put in touch with organizations and movements working to smash the State, Capitalism, and the Megamachine, just like our Na'vi role models did. Unfortunately, the link only led to a "page not found" message. So close to liberation, yet so far away.

What's It All About?

Which leads us back to our main point: why *Avatar* is the most important film in history. *Avatar* is the ultimate argument against having any faith in the dominant mass media as a means of inspiring opposition to the global system of domination. *Avatar*'s explicit message is that civilization is oppressive and destructive and that we should break with it, smash its power, and go to live in egalitarian, ecological communities instead. And it uses the most sophisticated CGI's in history to bombard the audience with this message. If one believes in the power of mass media (and who cannot today), one would expect its impact to be, on some level, quite enormous. It is not only scathing in its condemnation of imperialism in general, but quite specifically attacks the very rationales and strategies that have been used to instigate and carry out the war in Iraq and other recent conflicts. It's heavy-handed to the point of being transparently manipulative in depicting the devastation inflicted on tribal societies by imperialism, and specifically capitalist, profit-driven imperialism. Yet the film's ability to inspire any active opposition to war and imperialism is nil. In fact, never in the history of this world, or probably any other one, has any anti-war propaganda been so practically ineffectual.

However, this is not surprising, once we penetrate beneath the surface level of narrative and look at the various levels of meaning conveyed by the film. If we were to express it in Lacanian terms, we might say the following. On the imaginary level, there's an affirmation of the primitive, the wild, nature, the tribal, and the communal. Anarcho-primitivism. The *objet petit @*. Yet there is a contradiction here, because it is obvious that the director is entranced with technology, and he communicates this to the viewer powerfully on the imaginary level in the impressive military technology, the avatar/drone technology, and the mystified technology of the great primeval cybernetic forest. On the symbolic level, there are all sorts of contradictions. On the one hand, there is an affirmation of the civilized male hero (alias the White Messiah), his successful oedipal rebellion, and the phallic forces of technology and self-assertive force. But there is also an endorsement of excessive oedipal rebellion and an alliance with the mother (in the symbolic form of the pre-patriarchal feminine divinity) and against paternal power. On the level of the real (and this is where the real force of the film lies), there is an affirmation of the inexorable course of technological domination.

This structure of meaning can also be expressed in other, more explicitly politicized terms. We might also say that on the level of consumptionist imaginary, there is a gratification of the widespread fascination with nature, the wild, the primitive, the tribal. In this way, the consumptionist ego is gratified. On the level of the productionist imaginary, there is an appeal to the technological power and the strong male figure, the actor/creator. There's an irony here, since there is an explicit critique of technological and productionist ideology, at the same time that the technological and productionist imaginary are affirmed. On the level of the social reality underlying the imaginary and ideology, there is an affirmation of the course of the system of domination. The blue people are obviously living in fairytale land, a world that has no real connection to planet earth. The white male hero and his blue hybrid avatar/drone also inhabit an alien world, the world of cinematic myth that is alien to any conceivable real–world action. The one thing that seems overpoweringly real in this film is the machinery. It's entirely plausible that something quite like it will be around in the relatively near future. The film presents a realistic extrapolation of what is now taking place. Even the avatar, the eponymous hero of the film, is an extrapolation of the prosthetic bodies that are now evolving and, most significantly, of the drone technology that is becoming so central to global domination.

The Apotheosis of the Drone

And this points to one of the most profound levels of meaning in *Avatar*. In a multitude of ways, it reinforces the ideology of technological domination that it seemingly questions. For example, it acts as ideology by perpetuating the illusion that technological development can continue in full force in the wake of devastating ecological catastrophe on earth. Jake describes "the world we come from," in the following terms: "there's no green there. They killed their Mother, and they're gonna do the same thing here." Apparently, mass extinction continued until there was not a single tree or bush left. Nevertheless, we find that not only has humanity survived, but also that Capitalism has flourished and is moving on to new conquests across the universe. No doubt, the DJIA hovers quite comfortably in the seven-figure range. Given its initial plot premises, *Avatar* would have delivered a more authentic ecological message if its entire cast of human characters had been non-existent.

But the most powerful ideological message is in the Apotheosis of the Drone. As the Empire moves in for the kill, the Na'vi are reduced to the point of "Only a God can save us," or, perhaps, "Only a God, with the help of its avatar, can save us." On the most overt level, it is, as Brooks and Žižek point out, the latest incarnation of the White Messiah that saves them. On a deeper level, it is, ironically, the Drone, the latest product of the drive for technological domination in the service of Capital, that saves them. This unacceptable solution is in the end negated, as the Drone is transformed into a "real" Na'vi and the human substrate disappears, but this is only magical negation. According to the central narrative, the drone is still a drone, and salvation is achieved through the process of becoming-drone. Thus, the Drone is the final truth of *Avatar*. And it is whatever God it is that lies behind the Drone, not Eywa, that is its true Deity. If we want to define this Deity's nature more precisely, we must say that it is a Triune God. The Three Natures of this Trinity are called Capital, State, and Technique. It is the God whose name cannot be spoken in the film, but Who is present everywhere. This is the real Divinity that is incarnated in the avatar.

Do You Get It?

So how precisely does the fantasy-structure of *Avatar* operate? The film goes one imaginary step beyond even a fundamentally fundamental-fantasy-themed film like *Lost Highway,* in which much of the plot consists of elements of a personal fantasy. In *Avatar,* almost the *entire* film consists of such a fantasy. There are various elements of the real: a protagonist with a real wrecked body; a real dead brother; and a real dying planet. There is also the real of political and economic power, represented by the Corporation, its Army, and its technology. The rest is the clash of fantasies. Jake's dead brother signifies his own dead ideal self, so his opportunity to animate his twin brother's avatar and live through it is a fantasy of resurrection, and ultimately a fantasy of salvation through the power of technology. A fundamental fantasy that is perhaps central to the film's plot is the fantasy that we can save ourselves if we can find and appropriate some X that is somewhere out there. In the current real-world version of that fantasy, the X is, above all, oil. So a useful thought-experiment would be to substitute "oil" for "Unobtainium" in some of the key lines of the film.

   Cameron realizes (like a large segment of humanity does, to no effect) that the gratification of this particular fantasy amounts to killing the planet to save it, so within his alternative fantasy world the contradictory quality of conventional fantasy is made ludicrously explicit. The X that will save us is called "Unobtanium." Even when you get it, you don't get it. But strangely, no one in the film seems to get it. It's just left as blatant Romantic irony, and is thus one of the most appealing touches in the film (the tiniest bit of surreality that hints that Cameron and everyone involved in this project might not be totally depraved). The concept of "Unobtainium" is, implicitly, a scathing judgment on a society based on

The Empire is driven by a desire that drives it to destroy
anything, including itself, in order to satisfy that desire.

the technofix. The Empire is driven by a desire that cannot possibly be fulfilled. An insane fundamental fantasy based on that desire drives it to destroy anything, including itself, in order to satisfy that desire. This judgment is, of course, contradicted by the film itself as a technologically utopian project, and by its plot elements that involve either explicit or mystified technological liberation. The concept of "Unobtainium" is perhaps also an inadvertent expression of the Lacanian conception of desire, that the very unobtainable nature of the object of desire is basic to the functioning of desire and jouissance. This conception is, however, also contradicted in a big way by the film itself, which culminates in a utopia of full gratification. We might say the substance of the "Mystical Body" of Eywa is revealed in the end to be "Obtainium." So, in the end, the film ironically affirms precisely the same project that it negates: the solution to the problem of existence is to find and appropriate the X that is somewhere out there, but it turns out to be a spiritual substance, rather than a material one.

Another crucial difference from classic Lynchian fantasy, as expressed most clearly in *Lost Highway* and *Mulholland Drive,* is that despite their momentous social implications, the Lynchian fantasies retain the form of singular fantasies. Though viewers may sympathize with Fred Madison in *Lost Highway*, and perhaps fear elements of this character (the castrated Mad Son) in themselves, it is highly unlikely that anyone would desire to *be* Fred Madison. In *Avatar*, on the other hand, the protagonist's fantasy coincides with the fantasy that the film arouses in the viewer. It also coincides with a shared social fantasy that is reaffirmed by the film, but is inspired continually by the larger fantasy-world, the social imaginary. This is the fantasy in which reality is transformed through gestures rather than true acts. This might be through magical incantation, through acts of heroic will power, or, more mundanely, through voting for Democrats, in short, through anything other than the risk of the engaged act.

In the Beginning: The Logos

As was mentioned, it's always wise to keep an eye out for the purloined letter. And there is another amazing instance in which the letter is shockingly conspicuous, within the film itself. Rather astoundingly, the significance of the film, which is usually kept carefully hidden, is revealed very clearly in the *very first words* of the film. It states what everyone who views the film knows, but which is kept from consciousness by ideology and illusion. First, we begin with the real. Jake says he had "a big hole blown through the middle of [his] life." This expresses his subjective perspective, but it is grounded in objective fact, the course of Empire, the resulting necessity of war, the physical devastation of his body in war. Second, we move to his, and the film's, response to the real through the fantasy of freedom, the imaginary and illusory overcoming of the real. "I started having these dreams. . . . I was free." Third, and finally, we confront the failure of fantasy, the return of the real. "Sooner or later though, you always have to wake up." This has the ring of truth. You *always* have to wake up.

But the film contradicts itself on this very point. It presents us only with the *fantasy* of waking up, and thus helps prevent the viewers from waking up. *Avatar* takes the viewers into a dream world, a world of fantasy, in which one imagines being free, being able to act decisively, being able to defeat evil and transform the world. The protagonist wakes up from the fantasy-world of the Corporation and enters the even more fantastic fantasy-world of the Na'vi. There is no way that the viewers can follow him there. Eventually—specifically, when they leave the theater or turn off the DVD—they have to wake up from this fantasy. However, the deceptive moral and metaphysical injunction expressed at the end of *Avatar* is that we *don't* have to wake up from the fantasy, that we can go more deeply into it, that it will somehow be transubstantiated into the real. However, such moralism and metaphysics remain enclosed within the narrow walls of a transient fantasy. What is unstated is that when we wake up, from that fantasy, we wake up to another fantasy, the dominant fantasy, the one from which "you don't have to wake up." The one you can, and almost certainly will, go on living.

Every fantasy element of *Avatar* must be reread keeping in mind the dialectic between this dimension, the film's escapist fantasy world, and the dominant fantasy world in which the audience lives its life—and which is reflected more in the world of the Corporation than that of the Na'vi. For example when Jake is in the "link unit," a little outpost of empire that transports him to Na'viland, he observes, "Everything is backwards now. Like out there is the true world, and in here is the dream." However, this poses the real question: For the viewer, which is the most powerful dream, which is the dream that is taken for reality? On the one hand, when Home Tree is bombed, an eminently believable familiar element of the real world intrudes into the film. As Col. Quaritch says, "That's how you scatter the roaches." And this is, indeed, precisely how they scatter the roaches, and any other unfortunate insects that hang around with the roaches. On the other hand, the Na'vi, as the word implies, are the naïve, and their world is a world that is only credible to the naïve, but which is entirely implausible from the standpoint of society's fundamental fantasy, fundamental ideological fiction, fundamental facticity, and fundamental institutional framework. None of the audience can really believe that they could follow Jake's example when he joins the Na'vi, the naïve, except maybe the pre-teen members of the audience, and they will soon give up their innocence and become normally cynical teenagers.

One might ask how a viewer, especially a young male viewer who is part of the prime target audience, might realize the fantasy of flying on a Big Bird like our blue hero Jakesully? Certainly not by joining the long, slow struggle of grassroots eco-defense. *Avatar*'s fantasy world will not inspire them to join the fight against mountain top removal in West Virginia or ancient forest defense in the Pacific Northwest. No, the most promising option is to forget the boring idea of defending primeval forests and join the United States Air Force. That's the real way you get to fly the Big Bird (and, incidentally, wear a blue uniform). When one leaves the fantasy world of the theater and returns to the real world of the dominant imaginary, the dominant ideology, the dominant ethos, the dominant institutions, nothing is easier than to forget the ecological and primitivist moralizing and live the more meaningful elements of the fantasy—the parts that play into the dominant fantasy, the reigning social imaginary. Riding flying dinosaurs in Fantasyland is a good theme for a poster to put up in your room. It's not a good career choice.

Military Strategy in Pandorastan

Na'vi military strategy is a joke. Despite Cameron's occasional nods to "the Wisdom of the East," the plot shows that he knows nothing about how tribal peoples and peasants have resisted the state. Laozi expressed it well over two thousand years ago. "'I dare not take the offensive but I take the defensive; I dare not advance an inch but I retreat a foot.' This means: To march without formation, To stretch one's arm without showing it, To confront enemies without seeming to meet them, To hold weapons without seeming to have them."[11] The Na'vi do just the opposite. They confront vastly superior power head-on. They run out of the woods and shoot arrows at military megamachines. And remember, this takes place during a protracted period of conflict with the imperial military machine, so the Na'vi must have known something about the enemy. No wonder they need help from a honky. They're nothing but a honky hallucination of what indigenous people are like. It's said that after valiantly fighting the Spanish conquerors with wooden swords for a while, the Inca warriors sat down on the battlefield and allowed the invaders to hack them to death with their metal swords. They may have lost, but they would not lose as idiots. The Na'vi, on the other hand, fight exactly like idiots. Nevertheless, the plot requires that these idiots must win, so ultimately we have to become the idiots and swallow the plot. The Corporate Capitalist Military Machine is even more unbelievable. We are to believe that the Empire's military technology has gotten to the point that it can engineer complex humanoid organisms that are remote-controlled so precisely that they can do everything from fight prehistoric monsters to have sex with ten-foot tall blue aliens. We are

11. *Daodejing*, Wing-Tsit Chan translation, Ch. 69: 1-2.

then to believe that Na'vi arrows are strong enough to go through the heavily reinforced windows of cockpits of planes. We are to believe that its massive high-tech aircraft are so dependent on obsolete technology (and humans who can't shoot) that the aliens can hop on angry versions of Big Bird and actually fly close enough to slaughter the crew with arrows or even blow up the aircraft with hand-grenades. We are to believe that the best army the Corporation can buy has forgotten to order computer-guided missiles and chooses instead to fight off attackers at close range with hand-held machine guns. We are to believe that the satellite imaging somehow doesn't manage to pick up a counter-attack by thousands of rampaging dinosaurs. Satellites are already advanced enough to read license plates. Too bad for the Empire that the dinosaurs didn't have license plates on them.

The whole thing screams "fake."[12] The film's technological message is so powerful and unmistakable that even the dullest viewer will recognize, albeit subconsciously, that in any realistic *Avatar*-world many technological generations ago the whole fleet would have been turned into remote-controlled drones with computer-guided, precision-targeting weapons. The story would have come to an abrupt end when

12. The adoption of one simple interpretative assumption would save *Avatar* from such ridiculousness. The implicit theme of the film is the triumph of sophisticated technology. Merely interpret the film in a manner that is fully consistent with this theme and the narrative becomes rational and coherent. Pandora is a highly advanced technological utopia in which sophisticated technology pervades every aspect of its world. It is, in fact, stated quite clearly in the film that the whole planet is like one huge, complex computer network. This key bit of information is revealed in the following description of Pandora: "It's a network—a global network…they can upload and download data." We can obviously assume that the Pandorans have perfected military technology and are invincible in war. When they are faced with invasion, one of their technologies—let's call it "the Neuron Bomb"—generates a field of energy that distorts the enemy's perceptions. It causes them to perceive the Pandoran technological environment as pristine, wild nature, the Pandorans as simple savages, and Pandoran weapons as primitive bows and arrows, etc. (The audience is presented with this systematically distorted world but it is assumed that they are too intelligent to take it literally). Thus, the enemy, under the sway of the Empire of Electronic Illusion, completely underestimate the Pandorans and are doomed to defeat. The Pandorans vanquish the Earthling army, as the film recounts, but, given this added layer of meaning, their victory actually makes sense. Jake Sully, the one Earthling who is allowed into Na'vi society, finally discovers the truth behind the illusion. It is revealed to him shortly after the advanced Pandoran neurophysics technology downloads his mind into a new body. In other words, he gets the news shortly after the end of the film.

The irresistible Power of the Drone is the Message of the Real in Avatar.

Jakesully and the whole Na'vi community were blown into oblivion in the first assault by the SuperDrone "Enola Obama."[13] The implicit message of this War of the Worlds is crystal-gazingly clear. Blue-monkey lovers and other dissidents are dead meat. If you want to escape the path of the imperial juggernaut, be sure to smoke something very strong, chew a worm, or get bitten by an arachnoid, because that's the only way out.

Meet the Real Hero

Which is why the Drone is the real hero of the film. The Drone reveals the *telos* of superpower military-industrial technology. Human and cybernetic powers are increasingly transferred to the technological instrument at a distance, so that maximum destructive power can be achieved, combined with minimal risk to human and technical resources of the dominating power. In addition, the dominated can be more intensely terrorized while the dominators are rendered less and less vulnerable (though fantasies of vulnerability paradoxically increase as tolerance of risk declines). More rational, technocratic Democrats advanced this development more successfully than the crazier, more heavy-handed, and more overtly bellicose Republicans. Examples are Clinton's strategy of depending heavily on bombing campaigns using high-altitude, nearly invulnerable stealth aircraft, and Obama's geometrical increase over Bush in the use of drones. Avatars are the fantasized full realization of the potentials of this drone technology. The irresistible Power of the Drone is the Message of the Real in *Avatar*.

Of course, according to the surface narrative, magic—the magic of nature—takes over the technology in the end. We see a new twist on the *Deus ex machina* trick. Instead of the God arriving in the machine, the Goddess, Eywa, goes into the machine, the Avatar/Drone. Then presto, it's no longer a machine, or at least we're supposed to forget that it's a machine. Ultimately, this is the escapist fantasy message of *Avatar*. Forsake our nature, forsake the earth. It's lost and we're lost. The only refuge is a fantasy world in which we escape from our bodies and from

---

13. A satirical cartoon video on YouTube called "Avatar: How It should Have Ended" depicts the film as ending with the Corporate military finally remembering, just as it blasts off, that it has advanced weapons. It decides to nuke Pandora into oblivion. "Game Over!" The video has over 8.3 million hits so far and has gotten about 27,000 "likes' as opposed to about 3,500 "dislikes."

our world. However, the fantasy message fades to the degree we face the Message of the Real (as we, that is, the non-psychotics among us, must). We all know that the technology is real and the fantasy is a total fake.

Avatar is not the only recent film to that revolves around the future of drone technology. This theme is explored brilliantly in the Mexican film *Sleep Dealer*, a neglected masterpiece of techno-dystopian cinema. In it, we see a world in which technologies have been invented to allow workers to perform virtual labor at distant sites. First, the workers have terminals implanted in their bodies, after which they can be hooked up to advanced cybernetic systems to do virtual/real labor. The workers go through the motions of labor in dismal warehouses in Mexican border towns, while the actual labor is carried out by remote-controlled robots in L.A., Phoenix, Denver, etc. It's a dream come true for racist, imperialistic capitalism. The Empire can import not only the products of cheap Mexican labor, but also the cheap labor itself, without having a single Mexican set foot on American soil. The film also brings in more traditional drone technology, since economic domination is enforced by remote-controlled bombers. Its real brilliance is to reveal prophetically a future in which military drone technology is combined with a system of drone production. What *Sleep Dealer* presents in a clear and devastatingly critical way, *Avatar* presents in a thoroughly mystified, deceptive, and ideological form. The future world is a world of domination by the Drone. If we fight against this domination, we may win or we may lose. But in order to fight against it, we need to recognize clearly, on the material, ideological, imaginary, and practical levels, the precise nature of the enemy. *Avatar* does everything it can to create obstacles to such consciousness.

Please Close Your Mind on the Way Out

So, what have we learned from *Avatar* about how to resist the Empire? Apparently, that you're in good shape if you're skilled at doing magic and riding prehistoric monsters. Unfortunately, there are no prehistoric monsters around, and magic, though it has its place in any decent culture, has already been tried as a military strategy. There were attempts In the 60's to levitate the Pentagon, and, while some people had fun trying, it just didn't work. Science is already making us post-human, and as *Avatar* tells us, if you can just find a magic tree, you get to be *post*-post-human. But, of course, you won't find that elusive tree, and you won't do the double negation trick. When, at the end of the film, "the aliens" go "back to their dying world," we find another point at which *Avatar* tells us the brutal truth, albeit on a slightly metaphorical level. For this is precisely where the earthlings go when they exit the theater, leaving the fantasy world of Pandora far behind them.

Le Chaos, ou l'Origine du Monde

Le Chaos, ou l'Origine du Monde, The Temple of Muses Bernard Picart, (1673-1733)

5

THE PASSION OF THE MASOCHRIST

Coming Attraction: The Passion of the Buddha?

It's rumored that Mel Gibson has been hired to do for Buddhism what he's done for Christianity. His next film will be *The Passion of the Buddha*. Do you know the story? The Buddha's end also came through a sacrifice. A lavish banquet was prepared for him but one of the dishes was contaminated. Knowing this, and having consideration for his host and companions, the Buddha chose to eat the poisonous food and leave the wholesome dishes for the rest of the assembly. What followed is rather harrowing—but imagine the vast cinematic possibilities. Twelve hours of vomiting, diarrhea, excruciating pain, and intestinal bleeding. Though the scriptures remain discretely reticent on this subject, there was no doubt abundant and painful gas. In short, the stuff that Mel Gibson movies are made of.

Somehow I doubt whether many Buddhists would find this drama very compelling. However, there may be among them a few naive souls with a pathologically morbid fear of being reincarnated as a slug who might think it could do them some good. If the film materializes, we will certainly investigate this question carefully. Meanwhile, we will be content to take a look at Gibson's first stab at a passion story.

Stephen Duplantier

Take and Eat. . .

As I entered the theater I felt immediately that this was a strange
ambience for what I had been told was a deeply religious experience.
No incense wafted through the atmosphere, but there was a pervasive
fragrance of butter. This was no eucharistic feast but there was a whole
lotta eatin' goin' on! Did the sin of gluttony go out with usury?

The Crucifixion had to wait for a long series of trailers. A collection
of cinematic factoids. A short exhorting the audience to "put an end
to piracy" with a moving description of the heroic efforts put in to
cinematic car chase scenes that should not go un- or under-rewarded.
A slapstick vignette from the American Express Corporation about
blowing up gophers. A comic episode, starring a bear and dedicated
to the greater glory of Hershey's Chocolate. An offer of the entire
Matrix saga on DVD. A grotesquely obscene Coke ad (actually a mock-
eucharist) about the unification of humanity through the distribution of
colored sugar-water by a benevolently beaming black lady who incants
"I wish I could share all the love in my heart" while actually sharing
nothing more than colored sugar-water that is not in the real world
shared but actually *sold* to many millions of the wretched of the earth
at a rather exorbitant cost. Feeble adolescent humor, delivered by actual
adolescents who probably know better, on behalf of Movietickets.com.
Previews of *Agent Cody Banks*, *Two Brothers* and *Spiderman*. A futile
plea for the audience members to turn off the cell phones (a big question:
when Jesus asks "Father why hast Thou forsaken me?" will one of those
damn phones go off, as if the answer has finally arrived?) And, assuming
that this generally husky congregation hungered and thirsted for more
than righteousness, one more plug for visiting the concessions for a final
dose of buttered popcorn and colored sugar water.

Finally, as the result of our purgatorial efforts in enduring this
mild but seemingly interminable torture, we are informed that "Icon
Productions" and "New Market Films" are ready to reward us with the
blood and gore (and who knows, maybe the salvation) we've come here
for.

Hippie, Skinhead, Whatever

When Jehovah's Witnesses and Mormons come to my door, I
sometimes greet them with, "No thanks, I already have a mythology."

Well, it's more or less the same product that's on sale here. Somehow most of the commentators on this film, even those who are vaguely troubled by it, haven't quite caught on. Most reviewers have either let it pass for "history," or criticized it to varying degrees as inaccurate or somewhat misguided history.

Mel Gibson certainly made a heroic effort to create the illusion of historical authenticity. The actors worked for months on their lines in Aramaic and Latin. And Mel Gibson's Jerusalem was not rebuilt in Rome in a day. No, his army of slaves labored mightily to construct a 2 ½ acre set, including a temple, a courtyard, a praetorium and Pontius Pilate's palace, at Cinecittá Studios, while the outdoor scenes were shot in the ancient Italian town of Matera in the south. Never before have so many done so much to make things seem so old. But despite all this impressive imagineering, it's not history. The product is pure mythology. And the specific brand of the product is *blood sacrifice mythology*. It's the brand typical of ancient barbarism, and has fueled a multitude of barbarisms ever since—even to the present.

Despite the raves of the local movie reviewers and church bulletin writers, the experts have pretty well dissected the claims of authenticity. Take Jesus, for example. Physical anthropologist Joe Zias, an expert on the ancient Near East, notes that Gibson's Jesus is long-haired, as he's depicted in Western religious art and popular culture, whereas Jewish men of the period in reality had short hair. He also explains that neither Jesus nor his cross-totin' helper would have been able to carry the whole cross as depicted by Gibson. The thing might have weighed as much as 350 lbs.! If Gibson really wanted to salvage the scene he would have to change the title to *The Passion of the Hulk* and maybe call in Arnold. In real crucifixions, the upright support stayed in place at the execution site, and the victim only carried the cross bar. Furthermore, if Jesus' hands were nailed as in Gibson's film, the weight of his body would have torn them from the nails, and the Roman soldiers would be mocking Jesus for continually falling off the cross. In reality, crucifixions took place at busy crossroads, so that the victims could be made an example, rather than on a remote hillside that fit Gibson's dramatic intentions better. Finally, "victims of this form of state terror were always stripped naked whereas here the actor is clothed."[1] Presumably, historically accurate nudity would be taboo for Gibson and his cult, while something like the

---

1. Joe Zias, "The Mel Gibson Controversy—A Postscript" at http://www.joezias.com/MelGibsonControversy.com.

historically unverifiable reduction of Jesus's flesh to the consistency of an uncooked Big Mac patty is no threat to their sense of the obscene. In short, to hell with history, we're in the world of sado-masochistic fantasy and blood sacrifice mythology.

What about the extraordinary effort at authenticity involved in having the actors memorize their lines in Latin and Aramaic? Well, Gibson's Latin-speakers should really have been speaking Greek to be accurate. Also, the Latin is completely wrong for the period, since in the film church Latin rather than classical Latin is used. This was convenient, since it's pronounced like Italian, the language of most of the actors, but it didn't even exist in Jesus's day. Biblical scholar Bruce Chilton summarizes just how bad it all is. "In fact, the Semitic-language scenes are a wild brew of Aramaic, Hebrew, and Syriac with grammatical mistakes in all three. The Latin is pretty good, but to have Jesus conversing learnedly with Pilate in that language is just too funny for words. There is not a word of Greek in this film, not even in the titulus on the cross, although John's Gospel specifies that the charge against Jesus was written in Greek (19:20) as well as in Latin and Aramaic."[2] A rumor has it that Gibson's advisors informed him that based on solid focus group data he could probably get away with a placard saying "Esusjay of Asarethnay, Ingkay of the Ewsjay," but he rejected it as a little too chancy.

Gibson's theory seems to be that authenticity is in the eye of the beholder—and in the ear of the uncomprehending hearer. If it's some kind of Aramaic, that should be enough. Who cares if the Aramaic sounds like the English in old war movies that's spoken with ludicrously heavy German accents so that we can pretend that we're actually hearing German. In Mel Brooks' *History of the World Part I* the French peasants complain that the aristocrats took everything from them—even their language. As they lament, "We just have this stupid accent!" In *The Passion*, the Romans apparently left the natives with their language, but they *still* ended up with lousy accents. Which only proves that Mel

---

2. Bruce Chilton, "Mel Gibson's Passion Play" at http://www.bibleinterp.com/articles/ Chilton_Passion.htm. This brilliant and erudite review is the best thing I've seen on the film. It's scandalously funny, a stumbling block to all future efforts to satirize this film. Chilton encapsulates the essence of the film's degraded aesthetics and warped ideology in his terse observation on its anti-climactic climax: "[Jesus's] immaculate linen shroud trembles in the breeze, awaiting shipment to Turin." Chilton also notes that Gibson seems to have gotten his image of what stoning was like more from Monty Python's *Life of Brian* than from historical accounts.

Brooks himself should definitely have done this movie. The Romans could have spoken English with an Italian accent, the Jews with a Yiddish accent, and Jesus, as the only *half-non-Earthling* in the script (it's a fact!), could have spoken like Mr. Spock.

Much has also been made not only of the ersatz historicity of the film, but also of its supposed "faithfulness" to the Scriptures. But that's far from the truth. Gibson's many revisions and insertions have been pointed out, including the padding of a number of scenes with material that comes not from Holy Writ but from the writings of the anti-Semitic German nun, Anne Catherine Emmerich (1774-1824). In her book of meditations and visions, *The Dolorous Passion of Our Lord Jesus Christ*,[3] she includes numerous anti-Semitic passages, including one in which she has a vision of an episode in Hell in which we discover that "Satan desired the crime of the Jews."[4] In another passage that might well have inspired some of Gibson's scenes, she observes that "the sight of [Jesus's] sufferings, far from exciting a feeling of compassion in the hard hearted Jews, simply filled them with disgust, and increased their rage. Pity was, indeed, a feeling unknown in their cruel breasts."[5]

Let's consider some other glaring problems that are often overlooked concerning the relationship between *The Passion* and the New Testament accounts. Take the depiction of Judas. Some questionable points can be dispensed with quickly. For example, when he gets his thirty pieces of silver it's sent sailing through the air to him in slow motion from about twenty paces away. The camera follows it as it carefully homes in on its target. *Stee-rike!* (though Judas bungles it a bit). OK, dramatic license, since the Bible doesn't say exactly how it was presented to him. But after this, Gibson shows Judas giving the thirty pieces of silver back and then going away to hang himself, as the *Gospel of Matthew* indeed recounts. But in the *Acts of the Apostles* Judas doesn't give it back at all, but instead buys a plot of land with his accursed silver. After which he falls down. He splits open. His guts gush out. Actually this is a much more interesting story and just gory enough to delight a Mel Gibson—who nevertheless omits it, as he omits all the other variations of the New Testament stories.

To be really faithful to Scripture, Gibson would have had to do a sort of Rashomon-style story, offering the viewer the various conflicting

3. The text can be found online at http://www.emmerich1.com/DOLOROUS_PASSION_OF_OUR_LORD_JESUS_CHRIST.htm.
4. Ibid., p. 123.
5. Ibid., p. 171.

Biblical accounts of what happened to Judas, what Jesus' last words were, whether there was an earthquake, when exactly Jesus was resurrected, etc. As it is, he sides with just *one* of the accounts, possibly giving the viewer the impression that the others might actually be wrong. Pretty close to blasphemy, I'd say![6]

Despite all the hype about historical accuracy and loyalty to Scripture, Gibson himself admitted that he had an ax to grind in the film: "This is my version of what happened, according to the gospels and what I wanted to show—the aspects of it I wanted to show."[7] So he had this ax, and it ends up as a very bloody one, as we shall see, in the course of his religious crusade.

Addiction and Crucifixion

What exactly is the religious outlook that forms the basis for Gibson's image of *The Passion*? It's a reactionary form of Catholicism, but that generic description hardly does it justice. It's roots go far back in Gibson's life. While he's widely thought to be Australian he was actually born in Peekskill, New York[8] in 1956 and raised there until the age of twelve, when his father, Hutton Gibson, took the family to Australia. The faith of his father is Mel's model for his version of ol' time Catholicism. Hutton Gibson is a "Sedevacantist," a term derived from the Latin for "empty seat." The Sedevacantists believe that every Pope since John XXIII has been illegitimate (in the legalistic, and not necessarily the parental, sense). Don't try to explain to them the ridiculousness of their position; they'll just give you that Sedevacant stare in return. Critics claim that Hutton's Sedevacantism also encompasses anti-Semitism and Holocaust denial.

For much of his life, Gibson didn't quite grasp the profundities of the Sedevacantist *Weltanschauung*. But then things got really bad and his father's cult started to look increasingly good. Gibson reports that as a result of a way-out-of-control life with excesses of drugs and alcohol, he

---

6. See Steven Elliot, "The Death of Judas" at http://home.austin.rr.com/selliott4/papers/judas.html for a fascinating account of how some fundamentalist interpreters actually try to construct a single script that includes all the contradictory elements, with results that are both literalist and a bit surrealist at the same time.

7. "Excerpts from ABC News/Primetime correspondent Diane Sawyer's interview with Mel Gibson, February 16, 2004" at http://www.beliefnet.com/story/140/story_14044_2.html.

8. Yes, "peeks kill"—a bizarrely ironic birthplace for someone accused of promoting a voyeuristic attitude to violence and death.

reached a low point over a decade ago. "I would get addicted to anything, anything at all. Okay? Doesn't matter what it is ... drugs, booze, anything. You name it—coffee, cigarettes, anything. Alright?"[9]

Alright, we got it! The obvious solution was fundamentalist religion—addicts usually pick up any convenient drug if it's lying nearby on the shelf. And it's perfect for the addictive personality since it's all about abject dependency. That's why it's proven to be such a great cure for addictions in so many tough cases. It's like methadone addiction as a cure for heroin addiction. Well, Gibson desperately needed some kind of cure. He says that he finally even contemplated throwing himself out of a window. Instead, he turned to the Bible—and apparently threw *it* out of the window after finding a few useful ideas. In reflecting on his conversion experience he concludes that "pain is the precursor to change, which is great . . . That's the good news."[10] In Gibson's hands it's not exactly the Good News in what some might think of as the Gospel sense. Maybe the truth is that a lot of pain led Mel Gibson to change Jesus into what Gibson needed him to be: a bloody icon produced on behalf of regressive fundamentalist religion.

Which is what he has put a lot of his own personal effort into creating. For example, he built his own little ultra-traditionalist Catholic chapel and has pre-Vatican II Latin Masses said there. Gibson said "I'm just Roman Catholic, the way they were up until the mid '60s."[11] But of course Roman Catholics were no more one way before the mid '60's than everybody was one way before the way-out '60's changed like everything man.

Gibson thinks that those ol' time Catholics were really tough-assed. In an interview with *The New Yorker* he said that not only benighted pagans and cursed infidels but also misguided heretical Christians like his own wife (if she doesn't clean up her spiritual act) are damned to Hell.[12] Elsewhere he says that she deserves a medal for helping him with his addiction. I wonder if people get to wear their medals in Hell? What's the correct Sedevacantist position on this one?

Leading man Jim Caviezel, by the way, shares Gibson's Catholic

---

9. "Pain and *Passion*: Mel Gibson Tackles Addiction, Recovery and the Controversies Over His New Film" at http://abcnews.go.com/sections/Primetime/Entertainment/mel_gibson_passion_040216-1.html.

10. Ibid.

11. Frequently Asked Questions About Mel Gibson's *Passion*" at http://www.beliefnet.com/story/140/story_14087_2.html.

12. Jeannette Walls with Ashley Pearson, "Mel Gibson says his wife could be going to hell" at http://www.msnbc.msn.com/id/4224452/.

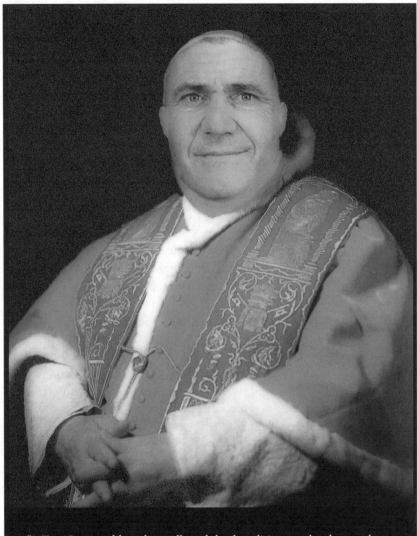

"A True Pope could not have allowed the demolition to take place or those with the dynamite to remain. How was it that an anti-Church, anti-Christ was able to usurp Ecclesiastic power and sit on Peter's throne? Who knows? We do know that it was prophesied to occur. We do know that the Catholic Church warned about it and tried to protect us from it. We can bet that Satan was at the controls."

--from a Sedevacantist website (www.holyromancatholicchurch.org)

Stephen Duplantier

fundamentalist faith. Caviezel, an authentic native of Washington State, is a pretty Aryan-looking choice for the role of long-haired Jesus. But with his blue eyes cinematically transubstantiated into brown, and his dark hair, he comes across as exotically handsome and of indeterminate if certainly European ethnicity. Caviezel reports that a crucial turning point in his life was a visit to the legendary village of Medjugorje in Bosnia, famous as the site of the Blessed Virgin Mary's repeated appearances for conversations with teenagers (why if the BVM was targeting teens she didn't do it through a more effective channel—MTV comes to mind—we'll probably never know). He reports that "I felt extraordinary peace and love there, in this little town of 300 families. The sun literally dances in the sky. It's the only place Slobodan Milošević couldn't get with his guns. They'd fly missions over this little town, try to drop bombs, and clouds would come up and they couldn't find it. That place led me to this role. It was Mary, again, who led me to do this."[13] If the teens asked the BMV why she let the bombs drop on the other villages, or why she let their citizens be herded into concentration camps, gang-raped, and slaughtered, Caviezel does not divulge her answer. Maybe she prefers to hang out in places with those "literally" dancing suns and smaller Muslim populations.

The Plot Thickens

Gibson proves that a plot can be wafer-thin yet thick headed at the same time. There *are* a few plot details beyond the central sado-masochistic theme. But in all of them, the treatment is heavy-handedly unimaginative, as I suppose authentic faith-based film initiatives have to be. The Bible says that Jesus was mocked, so mocking we get—and more mocking, and more mocking. While the hand washing of the white-washed Pontius Pilate is robbed of all irony, the plebian Roman troops, like the Jewish mob, come across as ignorant, sadistic louts who can't do much other than mock and brutalize. With a few noble exceptions, the Jews—especially the High Priests—are depicted as deeply and insidiously evil. We also get a glimpse of Herod's court, which is depicted as a sort of fundamentalist freak show. Herod appears to be gay, there's a morbidly obese woman, and an actual black person. More or less the late-50's popular misconception of a gathering of Beatniks.

The film gives lip service to "love your enemy," but the non-verbal

---

13. Gayle Macdonald, "Christ complex," at http://www.caviezelcountry.com/id118.htm.

communication is clear: these are enemies you can really love—to hate. The film is obsessed with mocking and thus betrays the deep fundamentalist fear of its absurdities being unmasked through humor, ridicule or satire. Like all kinds of dogmatism, fanaticism, and rigid domination, fundamentalism depends on maintaining a fragile, self-denying, grimly serious state of (un-)consciousness. That's why the "True Christian," the "Real Man," the "Red-Blooded American," and the "Proud White," as good as they are at laughing at others, seldom have a sense of humor and never have a sense of irony. So Gibson is out to get the mockers, and especially the Jewish mockers. Sometimes his Jews even mock when the mocking makes absolutely no sense. For example, when Jesus is accused of curing illness with the assistance of devils, the crowd comes out with a big guffaw, as if to say, "Yeah, like, *really*." But saying this would put them on *Jesus's* side, since they'd really be laughing at the High Priests' accusations, and thus defending him against these accusations. A non-brain-dead director or screenwriter would have had them shaking in their sandals instead.

But even the vicious and crude mockery of the crowds pales beside other more powerful images of evil. The classic imagery linking Woman-Nature-Evil is especially striking. This time Woman is not only a tool of Satan, she is Satan! The widely commented-upon "androgynous" Satan tilts decidedly toward the gynous side (and is played by Italian actress Rosalinda Celentano). At one point one wonders if the Demonic Lady's name might not be Philosophia, for she tempts Jesus with such questions as "Who is your father? Who are you?" These are precisely the questions that seem to have been at the center of the director's own crisis-ridden life. Is it his father's will that is finally being done? Has he found a self that is acceptable to his father and that he can finally be satisfied with?

But Satan lives far more in the world of the deeply and frighteningly irrational than in the realm of reason. There's a mock pietà scene in which the ghastly Satanetta cradles a grotesque Devil-Child, who chimes in with the general Jesus-mocking. Nature, on the other hand, is primarily the mute background for the human and superhuman drama. Except when it slithers out into full view as a ghastly serpent whose head is quickly crushed under Jesus's heel. But it's Ms. Satan who steals the show. She's by far the most attractive figure in this film. She lurks menacingly behind the scenes and then shocks the Hell out of you. Her weird, evil creepiness is infinitely more powerful than Jesus's divine wholesomeness. As the Crucifixion reaches its climax, she screeches out like a deranged rock star. Diabla! She deserves her own movie.

There are a few hints thrown in that Jesus may have had a life off the Via Dolorosa. There's a flashback to Jesus as a young carpenter. He just finished building a table and he hops up on it, apparently to check to see if it will hold him. First, I wondered how many tables collapsed while he was practicing before he found a good design. Then it occurred to me that if he did find a good design, why would he still be hopping up? But wait—maybe this was the first one that didn't collapse. But this still doesn't work because if he's God, wouldn't he already know whether it would hold him? So why would he have to hop up? And if he could walk on water, wouldn't almost any table be strong enough to hold him? It's questions like this that try one's faith. There's also a little bit of Resurrection at the end, almost as a brief afterthought. Strangely, while the seeming thousands of wounds and scars have completely disappeared from Jesus' body, he still has holes in the palms of his hands. Are we to conclude that only hand-wounds are Resurrection-proof? Gibson can claim that he's just following tradition on this point, but

Resurrexit, sicut dixit.

Stephen Duplantier

having previously turned Jesus into more or less one big wound, the survival of only a couple of them seems particular absurd. Needless to say, there's no Ascension into Heaven. Let's be honest, Gibson just wasn't bravehearted enough to try it. With all the financial resources and cinematic technology at his disposal, he still didn't have the guts to take on the challenge of showing Jesus rising up into the stratosphere. This wouldn't just be falling into the carnivalesque, but even worse, into the Canaveralesque. State-of-the-art special effects would of course have precluded any need for those all-too-conspicuous strings that detracted from earlier efforts at staging the scene. But Gibson knew that whatever he might do, the audience would undoubtedly still see the strings he was pulling, suspecting that they were probably attached to those holes that he left in Jesus' palms.

The truth is that Gibson's attempts to portray Jesus are cinematically doomed from the outset. This discussion makes no pretense of being a detailed theoretical critique of the film, but if it were, I'd point out that the downfall of the film was the director's adoption of a fundamentalist concept of incarnation that's aesthetically and dramatically lethal. This is, so to speak, its cinematic *Original Sin*. There's an irreconcilable contradiction involved in an attempt both to mythologize and at the same time to humanize. If incarnation is the synthesis of the finite and the infinite, fundamentalist film Jesus incarnates precisely the failure to achieve that synthesis—in its place there's only a bad finitude and a bad infinitude held in suspension. Of course, there's always the possibility of a leap of faith that seeks to surmount all contradictions, even dramatic one, but in this case it's a leap into an abyss of bad taste.

No Justice, No Prince of Peace

Forget it, Gibson, Jesus don't play that. Not Cornell West's Jesus, anyway. According to theologian and political activist West, "we're living in the biggest empire since the Roman Empire. Now the underside of the Roman Empire is the cross. That's where political prisoners were put to death. Those that had the courage to act over against the powers that be. Now we are in the American Empire . . . the legatee of Constantian Christianity," the imperial religion of "the persecution of Jews and others." West asks Gibson if he's "really gonna talk about the empire that we're a part of now?" and Gibson answers, "No, I'm gonna give you sadomasochistic voyeurism." But West's Prophetic Christianity says to

Gibson's version of the Passion, "No way, Hosea." "No, not for my Jesus... I have reality shows for that," he points out.[14]

The religious left in general is appalled by the film, for much the same reasons as West. Tom Beaudoin, in one of the film's most unrelentingly negative reviews, "The anti-Christian *Passion of the Christ*," sums up the problem: the film "over-individualizes Christianity by divorcing Jesus' crucifixion from other crucifixions . . . we are kept from seeing the banality of his death as something suffered by thousands of other political prisoners in his day."[15] It's not that it has absolutely no "redeeming values" but that these values are drowned in a sea of blood. Somewhere within the two hours of torture there are a few minutes of love and forgiveness—there's even a radical Jesus who warns that those who live by the sword will die by the sword. And the policies of Empire in the Middle East really don't come over too well. But it's unlikely that American audiences as the result of this film will be overcome by any sudden impulse to "sell everything (or maybe even anything) they have and give it too the poor" or to throw their bodies in the way of the murderous armies of Empire. It's more likely that they'll accept with teary, mildly masochistic gratitude the fact that they've been ransomed, and remain righteously content to wallow in the fruits of Empire as they make plans to come back and watch *Agent Cody Banks* while stuffing their faces with buttery popcorn.

MasoChrist Beats AnarChrist

The film's few hints at Jesus the AnarChrist's utopian vision of justice and compassion are overwhelmed by the dominant images of Blood Sacrifice of the MasoChrist. The core of the narrative is the ransom theory much beloved by both retrograde ultra-traditionalist Catholics and reactionary Protestant fundamentalists. This film is a paradigm case of how the repressive forces of communication operate in the consumer society. Heavy-handed censorship is never really necessary. Despite the fears of the overly paranoid right, subversive images can safely be tolerated—Jesus could have safely spouted pacifistic slogans and could even have repeated his famous nasty comment about the slim

---

14. "Toni Morrison and Cornell West in Conversation," The Nation Institute, New York Society for Ethical Culture, March 24, 2004. Video on Free Speech TV.

15. Tom Beaudoin, "The anti-Christian *Passion of the Christ*" at http://ncronline.org/NCR_Online/archives2/2004a/031904/031904s.htm.

chances that the rich have of reaching Paradise. All that is necessary is a dominant message that overwhelmingly reinforces passive acceptance of That Which Is (what the AnarChrist would call "the World" and which includes most of what is called "the Church"). Mel Gibson's version fits the mold perfectly. Lip service to love and justice, center stage for the Blood Sacrifice—it's all been done for you, so revel in an emotional orgy. Big vicarious pain, big self-justifying gain.

Jesus the AnarChrist is overwhelmed by Jesus the MasoChrist. The justifiable uproar over the film's anti-Semitism has unfortunately obscured another problem with the film: that it's basically a glorification of sadomasochistic murder. It's a Catechism of Sadomasochism. According to the fundamentalist interpretation of the film—as the fundamentalists themselves explain it—it's about *Jesus* dying so that his Father would forgive *our* sins. In other words, it's about a father demanding the death of an innocent child for things the poor kid's not responsible for. God, what a role model! Even as I write I read in a story from the Associated Press reporting that a fundamentalist Christian mother in Tyler, Texas was acquitted of murder for stoning two of her home-schooled children to death and maiming a third. She did it for the very traditional, Biblically-correct reason that she was "divinely chosen by God to kill her children as a test of faith." She did show a bit of spiritual originality when she explained further that she was also chosen "to serve as a witness after the world ended."[16]

Interestingly, the mother was acquitted "by reason of insanity." Nevertheless, according to many reports, millions of fundamentalist Christians sit weeping through *The Passion* not at all because they are witnessing the depiction of the murder of an innocent person in the name of what can only be described as a completely bloodthirsty, vindictive, sadistic and *insane* Divine Tyrant. No, it's because this torture and murder are allegedly being done in the name of their own pathetic, wormlike, submissive selves (or at least the masochistic side of their sadomasochistic selves) according to the sane, rational logic of blood sacrifice. But Biblical scholar John Dominic Crossan's response seems much more humane, ethical and sane: "I do not believe in a God who could forgive gratuitously but actually does so only after Jesus has been beaten to a bloody pulp in our place. If I accepted . . . Gibson's vision of this savage God, I hope I would have the courage to follow Mrs. Job's

---

16. Lisa Falkenberg, "Mother acquitted of killing children," Associated Press (4/4/04).

advice: 'Curse God, and die' (2:9)."[17] In one of the most ill conceived moves in the film, Gibson has a divine tear fall dramatically from the sky (i.e., where God is) at the Crucifixion. Presumably we're supposed to conclude that the Cosmic Child-Killer is saying, "Sorry, kid, this is hurting me more than it's hurting you." But the whole point of it is that Jesus is the one who's getting hurt, specifically in order to *satisfy* the disgruntled Patriarch. And besides, as Mel should have realized, nobody has ever fallen for that line from a child-abuser.

This story of blood sacrifice is the overwhelmingly central one of the film. Not only do the few meager "love your enemies" passages get overwhelmed by the ransom theme, but the treatment of one of Jesus's actual enemies in the film speaks much more loudly than these compassionate words. When one of the thieves crucified next to Jesus mocks him, a raven flies down, lights on top of the cross, and pecks the thief's eyes out. Presumably, the bird was sent on this mission by the Heavenly Father, who decided that the thief needed a little torture and mutilation before dying. The words "love your enemies" begin to appear as hollow as the sockets of the poor thief's eyes. One could imagine a sequel to this film in which Gibson would cast Jesus a bit differently to unleash even more of the sadistic side of the director's sadomasochism. After all, despite the successful ransom proposition there's still a lot of Hell and Purgatory to work with. How about a triumphant Christus Rex putting the hurt on hapless sinners, especially those *mockers*? Gibson could call it *Jesus in Furs*.

Do Mel Gibson's cinematic abuses mean that there's no place for sadism, masochism, violence, or cruelty in film? Far from it—though I could imagine him giving sadomasochism a bad name for a long time to come. However, long ago Artaud in *The Theater and Its Double*[18] described a "theater of cruelty" that helps one understand the aesthetic, intellectual and spiritual obtuseness of efforts such as Gibson's *Passion* and suggests what a creative, living "cinema of cruelty" might be. Cruelty in Artaud's sense is the "will" and "blind appetite for life capable of overriding everything,"[19] as opposed to Gibson's nihilistic rejection of real life, real humanity and real nature. Rather than numbing us by depicting, as Gibson does, "the lives of a few puppets," it "wakes us up."[20]

---

17. John Dominic Crossan, "Hymn to a Savage God" at http://www.beliefnet.com/story/141/story_14143_1.html.
18. Antonin Artaud, *The Theater and Its Double* (New York: Grove Press, 1958).
19. Ibid., p. 103.
20. Ibid., p. 84.

Rather than reinforcing our reactive fears and prejudices, it "overturns our preconceptions" and "acts upon us like a spiritual therapeutics whose touch can never be forgotten."[21] Rather than ignoring living nature, it can "cause the whole of nature to re-enter the theater in its restored form."[22]

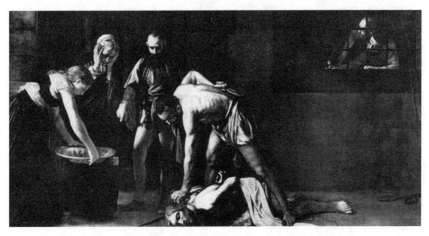

Jouissance sadique. Caravaggio's Beheading of John the Baptist, 1608

Rather than superficially playing with our sentiments, it is "unafraid of going as far as necessary in the exploration of our nervous sensibility."[23] Artaud contends that "the magical liberties of dreams" can only be "liberated" through a certain "cruelty and terror" that "probes our entire vitality, confronts us with all our possibilities."[24] For Artaud, there is a need to create what he calls "a metaphysics" (since he didn't have the word "surregionalism")—"a metaphysics of speech, gesture, and expression, in order to rescue it from its servitude to psychology and 'human interest.'"[25] The kind of "metaphysics" or anarchy of regionalities that a Grünewald or a Bosch can call forth in painting, and that a Pasolini or a Lynch can create (often with exquisite cruelty) in film. As Artaud says, this is far from any heavy-handed intrusion of metaphysical, much less religious, concepts but rather a more subtle "temptation of these ideas" through "humor with its anarchy" and "poetry with its symbolism and images." Religious directors *can* be exquisite poets and humorists—witness St. Alfred the Great. On the

21. Ibid., pp. 84-85.
22. Ibid., p. 86.
23. Ibid., p. 87.
24. Ibid., p. 86.
25. Ibid., p. 90.

other hand, look to a Mel Gibson for textbook examples of simplistic, reductionist psychology and morbid, self-indulgent, and ultimately inhuman "human interest."

Finally, what can we say about the description of Gibson's dramatically morbid and violent scenes as "Baroque"? Gibson himself has described the overt influence of the Italian Baroque painter Caravaggio on the staging of the film. He depicts the work that inspired him as "violent, dark, and spiritual."[26] This influence has often been cited; however there has been little comment on the degree to which Gibson's film is in a very technical sense a revival of the larger Baroque outlook and sensibility. The Baroque is characterized by extravagance and theatricality, the creation of striking and dynamic effects, a preoccupation with death and the transience of things, the breaking of conventions, naturalistic depictions, and an indulgence in emotional excesses. All of this describes perfectly Gibson's approach in *The Passion*. Moreover, Baroque aesthetic naturalism and emotionalism have been seen as a response to the counter-Reformation Council of Trent's call for more compelling depiction of religious truth in order to keep the faithful within the fold of the One True Holy Roman and Apostolic Church and to win back the apostates. Sounds amazingly like a description of Gibson's project!

Jesus in the Hands of an Angry Goy

Such august authorities as the film reviewer for the *New Orleans Times-Picayune* assure us that "charges of anti-Semitism" in this film "are completely unfounded." Imagine that: "completely." But *is* it anti-Semitic? As that well-known contemporary philosopher Bill Clinton once said "It depends on what you mean by 'is.'" Let's sidestep all the vicissitudes of the Problem of Being and just say this. Whatever may have been going on the director's mind, it *is* a film that objectively promotes anti-Semitism.

Gibson and his defenders have tried to refute this rather obvious fact. Pat Robertson, for example, notes that "it's important to remember that *The Passion* also has many positive portrayals of Jews."[27] He lists a number of these. Interestingly, there's one very glaring and telling

---

26. Holly McClure, "A Very Violent Passion," at http://www.nydailynews.com/front/story/54288p-50909c.html.
27. Pat Robertson, "An Intensely Personal Film" Beliefnet at http://www.beliefnet.com/story/141/story_14130_1.html.

omission in his list, The Big One. For Pat Robertson, "Jews" are always
the people around Jesus, not Jesus. Jesus is King of the Jews, but not
a Jew. For Pat, J.C. remains essentially an E.T. But let's get back to his
main point. There *are* some self-conscious attempts to counteract
the anti-Semitic aspects of the film. One of the characters with the
most stereotypically "Jewish" features carries the cross for Jesus and is
subjected to being contemptuously called "Jew" by the Romans. Oh,
we get it: some of Jesus's best friends were Jews. Haven't we heard that
one before? It just doesn't follow in any way that because there are a few
(and they really are few) positive images of Jews among the numerous
negative ones in a film that it isn't even *virulently* anti-Semitic, and much
less does it follow that the film does not *promote* anti-Semitism.

Gibson himself tries to explain the problem away. In response to
the question of who killed Christ, he replies "The big answer is, we all
did. I'll be the first in the culpability stakes here."[28] This "big answer" is
indeed important to the film, for without it the whole sado-masochistic
superstructure, built on the flimsiest of narrative bases, would come
crashing down. But unfortunately for Gibson's argument, his movie
also concentrates very heavily on the "little answer"—so heavily that
this answer can only be perceived by a great many viewers as a rather
enormous one.

Gibson says further that the film is not about "the blame game" but
rather about "faith, hope, love and forgiveness." Just as Clinton wondered
about the meaning of "is," you have to wonder what Gibson means by
the word "about." One thing is certain, it's *about* two hours and most
of that time is taken up with a story about a deliriously insane Jewish
mob, egged on by evil, monstrous Jewish leaders, torturing and lynching
a poor, innocent (extraterrestrial) victim. Well, I guess nobody could
possibly blame them, could they. How could such a silly idea *ever* arise in
anybody's mind?

In reality, Gibson's *Passion* is in an ugly tradition of depictions
of the Jews going back to medieval Passion Plays that have always
offered abundant ammunition to the ever-present anti-Semites and
Jew-baiters of Christendom. Tom Beaudoin notes that "none of the
primary Jewish characters on the 'good side' in the movie (Jesus or his
mother, for example) are portrayed with any easily identifiable 'Jewish'
characteristics, such as the prayer shawls that identify most of the Jews
on the 'bad side.'"[29] The notoriously anti-Semitic passage in which the

28. "Pain and Passion."
29. "The anti-Christian *Passion of the Christ.*"

Jewish mob shouts[30] "His blood be on us, and on our children" (Matt. 27:25) was dropped from the subtitles but remains in the sound track (in Aramaic). It took reports from focus groups for it to dawn on Gibson that including this classic proof-text for anti-Semites might be going a bit too far. Gibson commented to the *New Yorker* about dropping the subtitles that "if I included that in there, they'd be coming after me at my house, they'd come kill me."[31] And just who are these "they" that are out to "kill" Gibson at his first false move? Presumably it's not an angry mob of Aramaic speakers from the few villages where it survives today. But let's give him credit. At least he didn't say, "they'd crucify me."

Some have asked how, if the offending passage is in Aramaic, it could do any harm. True, if no one knows it's there, it would say more about Gibson's own anti-Semitic feelings than about the effects of the film. However, many viewers will, in fact, know. It's likely that versions used by anti-Semites (as will be discussed shortly) will have the subtitles restored. In any case, the inclusion of the passage in the sound track has itself created enough discussion that many viewers will know precisely what's going on in the scene.

Another suspicious aspect of the film is Gibson's contrasting depiction of the Roman and Jewish elites. He presents Pilate, entirely unhistorically, as a high-minded and conscientious ruler with a strong sense of justice. Pilate towers above the leaders of the Jews, depicted by Gibson as narrow-minded, despicable, and mean-spirited. Yet such first-century authorities as the philosopher Philo and the historian Josephus report Pilate to have been strong-willed and authoritarian. According to Philo "he was a man of a very inflexible disposition, and very merciless as well as very obstinate," noted for "his habit of insulting people, and his cruelty, and his continual murders of people untried and uncondemned, and his never ending, and gratuitous, and most grievous inhumanity."[32] As Cornell West sums it up, "Pilate was a gangster."

It's illuminating to look at some actual empirical evidence concerning the outlook of *Passion*-goers as compared to that of the general public. A poll from the Pew Research Center released on April 2 (unfortunately not April 1) said that a growing percentage of Americans—26%—believe that "Jews were responsible for Christ's death." Interestingly, 36% of

---

30. Yes, the mob. They all thought of this and shouted it out at exactly the same time!

31. Quoted in Garry Wills, "God in the Hands of Angry Sinners" *New York Review of Books*, vol. 11, no. 6 (April 8, 2004), p. 68.

32. "Between 'Passion' and Purim: Interview of Rabbi Brad Hirschfield by Rebecca Phillips," *Beliefnet* at http://www.beliefnet.com/story/141/story_14143_1.html.

those who have seen *The Passion* hold this view, (though a slightly higher than normal percentage already believed it before their indoctrination session). Among young people under thirty, the percentage holding this view has poisonously mushroomed over the past few years from 10% to 34%, while among blacks it has soared from 21% to 42%. It's disturbing that in all probability this means that an anti-Semitic collective blame mentality is growing, and that *The Passion* is feeding its growth.

If the film has verifiably had such an effect in the United States, what might its influence be elsewhere? Its reception in the Middle East is instructive. It was banned in Bahrain as "contrary to the Sharia, which prohibits the representation of the prophets." In Kuwait there's a battle between the Sunni majority, which supports its showing, and the Shiite minority, which wants to ban it. In Gaza and the West Bank pirated copies are selling well, as they no doubt will elsewhere, with or without additional subtitling.[33] The film poses a problem for certain radical Islamists. It's blatantly obvious to them (though intellectualistic, literal-minded Western liberals haven't caught on) that the film contains a healthy and very powerful dose of anti-Semitism—but it also contains images contrary to Islam. No doubt it's a tough dilemma, but as the history of religions testifies, when it comes to reconciling orthodoxy with hatred, consistency becomes a quite dispensable virtue.

Finally, I think that it's worth noting that at least one member of the Catholic hierarchy has heaped some fairly harsh criticism on Gibson's film. The Archbishop of Paris remarked with biting irony that the Gospel is "neither the Gallic Wars nor Napoleon's *Memoires*," and that "the love of God is not measured in liters of hemoglobin and spilled blood." The Archbishop sees Gibson's film as less a reflection of the Gospels than an expression of "the present epoch of violence and collective sadism."

If his response is atypical, the Archbishop is himself quite unusual among the Princes of the Church. He was born Aaron Lustiger in 1926 of Polish Jewish parents. He adopted Catholicism while being sheltered during the occupation/collaboration with a Christian family in Orléans. His parents were later deported by good Christians of a different tendency and died in the Holocaust. Cardinal Lustiger has been criticized for trying to "present the Shoah as a remake of the Crucifixion," an undertaking that runs its own risks. Yet it is noteworthy that he is accused, in other words, of promoting a confrontation between spirituality and real history with it's real suffering—exactly the kind of

---

33. *Libération* (April 2, 2004).

confrontation that Mel Gibson so scrupulously avoids, and one that drives the remythologizing Sedevacantists and their kind into their bunker-like chapels. It has been said that the Archbishop, who has made a memorial visit to Auschwitz, where his mother died, "has never ceased to be a Jew." In this he is quite unlike Mel Gibson's Jesus.[34]

"Dirty Jew"

Why Didn't Mel Play Jesus?

One might wonder, in view of Mel Gibson's delusions of grandeur and his insatiable desire for self-aggrandizement, why he didn't himself play Jesus in *The Passion of the Masochrist*. The answer is simple. Because he already played Jesus in *Braveheart*. And since he played it as both tragedy and farce at the same time, he didn't have to repeat the role. Besides, the only Savior that Mel would really want to play would be a Messiah of Murder and Mayhem, which is how he depicts his hero in *Braveheart*, William Wallace.

The overt text of the film deals with freedom and the evils of empire. However, the much more powerful subtext of Gibson's saga reeks of

---

34. "Mgr. Lustiger contre le 'sadisme' du film de Gibson," in *Le Monde* (3/26/04).

fascism and the subordination of the masses to a charismatic leader. Throughout the whole film, the Scots are incapable of doing a single half-way heroic or intelligent thing without the infallible guidance of their quasi-omnipotent, but ultimately martyred, lord and master. Not surprisingly, the film was a big hit with neo-fascist groups.

Scottish comedian Billy Connolly described the film as "a piece of pure Australian shite." This was probably the film's most perceptive one-word review, though to be fair, the great continent of Australia should hardly be blamed for Gibson's cinematic shite. Nevertheless, Connelly certainly put his finger on the quality of the product.

Philosopher Harry Frankfurt in his famous book *On Bullshit* describes the purveyor of that commodity as someone who "does not care whether the things he says describe reality correctly. He just picks them out, or makes them up, to suit his purpose." And as the *OED* says, "'shite' is basically bullshit, but worse." It's the kind of thing Mel Gibson would do.

Gary Oaks

WWJD

When the *London Times* published a list of the ten most historically inaccurate films, *Braveheart* was listed as number two. While Gibson will never make King of Scotland, and will certainly never qualify as King of the Jews, he's certainly the King of Cinematic Inaccuracy. Of the six most historically inaccurate films, two were directed by Gibson and in another he was the lead actor.

According to Gibson's travesty of history, William Wallace (who was not the historical figure called "Braveheart"), not only humiliated the English armies, but seduced and impregnated the King's daughter-in-law, Princess Isabelle, the future Queen of England. However, the Queen-to-be was only ten years old when Wallace died. Even if she was *d'origine française*, she couldn't possibly have been as precocious as Gibson makes her in the film.

For the sake of at least partial accuracy, Gibson should remake the film with the ten-year old Princess as his love interest. Since he claimed vociferously that he did all the historical research, it's conceivable that he was fantasizing that version the whole time, anyway. In any case, when, at the end of the film, Wallace is tortured on a cross, as his inspired followers look on, interspersed among a mob of blood-thirsty yahoos, it's rather clear what Gibson was fantasizing.

It Is Finished—Or Is It?

Some might think that in this review I've been playing Devil's Advocate. Not at all. As has already been pointed out, Satan acquits herself amazingly well in Gibson's courtroom drama and hardly needs my help. It's Jesus the Jew, once a victim of Roman imperialism, now the victim of this particular high-tech lynching, who can use any help he can get. So in conclusion and in all fairness, perhaps we should listen, as best we can, in our own way, to the condemned man.

What would Jesus do—if he came back? Somebody once said that "old Jesus would puke" if he could see what's going on today in his name. Perhaps, but as we discussed, the Buddha's more or less got that one covered. So what would he *really* do? Don't we all know, in our deepest, most righteous and compassionate heart of hearts, *exactly* what he would do? He'd go straight to the Mall, march into the theaters showing *The Passion of the Masochrist*, knock over the projectors, and scatter the buttered popcorn to the four corners of the earth.

Anonymous

Objet petit b—Beebz declared "more influential than Obama or the Dalai Lama."

6

GIANT ECONOMY-SIZE BROTHER

When the truth is found to be lies
And all the joy within you dies
Don't you want somebody to love?
--Jacques Lacan

This was Max Cafard's first article, from the Fall of 1984. It was a noteworthy achievement, because technically he did not exist at the time. Incidentally, the text predicts the fall of the Soviet Union five years before the fact, and foresees the coming triumph of the society of mass consumption in China. It is Cafard's most important prehumous, postposterous, work.—*Hieronymous Fisch*

Good News From The Free World

According to a Gallup Poll published in February of this fateful year, 1984, few people in the Free World believed that the "grim visions" of Orwell's fateful book, *1984*, "had come true." In a survey taken in six nations, most of his "predictions" were judged not to have materialized. At one extreme were the Germans and Swiss, who saw little evidence of Orwellian conditions in their well-organized countries. More ominous tendencies were noticed by the Americans, Canadians, and British. It was perhaps not a complete surprise that Brazilians, nearing over twenty years of military dictatorship, perceived some signs of the existence of an authoritarian State. However, even they were divided on whether such developments had progressed very far. In all countries, the greatest concerns were that government officials were living luxuriously at the expense of the majority, and that government snooping threatened personal privacy. No one seemed to be panicking because the Totalitarian Nightmare had become reality, or because its arrival was imminent.

The most interesting questions posed in the survey addressed conditions that already, without ambiguity, prevail in the contemporary world. Asked whether the government "uses false words and statistics to hide bad news about the economy and quality of life," only 40% of the Americans, 53% of Canadians, and 57% of the British expressed their awareness of these practices. A mere 12% of the Germans and 13% of the Swiss maintained this minimal contact with reality. Another telling question asked whether "the government urges people to surrender freedom in order to gain greater security." Given that every government of every state on earth requires people to surrender freedom in exchange for its brand of "security," a failure to respond positively indicates a remarkable ideological blindness. Yet, with the exception of Brazil's 35% (itself astoundingly low), the percentage of people expressing agreement was minuscule (ranging from 6% in Switzerland to 12% in Canada).

Despite all the discussion of *1984* in 1984, if one listened to the public, it was apparent that people felt pretty free in the Free World—even under Free World dictatorships. Or, this seemed to be the case if one looked merely at the literal responses. Perhaps the failure to get the correct "Orwellian" answers resulted from the fact that the major constraints on liberty in the contemporary period have not occurred in the classic Orwellian manner.

1984 Versus 1984

While some have lamented the "misuse" of Orwell's novel in the service of anti-communism, this criticism is misdirected. The inspiration for the work is, above all, Stalinism, and it depicts brilliantly the monstrous character of the totalitarian "socialist" State. Attempts to project the Orwel's model on Western societies, so that virtually everything takes on an "Orwellian" coloring, are doomed to fatuity. Of course, the West has something to learn from *1984*—it is a great work of literature and helps illumine important realms of human existence. Yet, its author makes no attempt to show any universally fated course of development for all modern societies. Big Brother is a striking symbol of authoritarian rule. But that particular Brother should not be taken as the dominant image of unfreedom in the contemporary Western World. In fact, that world has another despot who is an even more formidable foe. In the consumer society—the dominant form of advanced industrial society—our Brother is a much more agreeable fellow than was Orwell's.[1] It is the Commodity that rules above all other tyrants (and there are others in our oligarchy). In *1984* people could be driven to love Big Brother by the occasional frenzy of orgiastic political rituals. In difficult cases, they could be tortured into love. In 1984 (the real one), our Brother has no difficulty in capturing our affection. He is with us always as the ubiquitous object of desire.

The Contemporary Relevance Of 1984

The principal relevance of *1984* today can be summarized concisely: "$$$$." Anyone with any serious interest in the socio-political implications of the book has been studying such issues for some time. One did not have to wait for the magic year to arrive in order to explore its profundities. Ninety-nine percent of the academics who squeeze each word of the book dry of every ounce of portentousness have never

---

1. The identification of contemporary society as "consumer society" or "consumptionist society" indicates its most salient characteristic and points out the direction of its movement. Yet this is a vast oversimplification of a complex system. On the most general level, it underemphasizes the centrality of the technological and political spheres, which are profoundly conditioned by commodification, but remain irreducible. Furthermore, consumption is itself dependent on the realm of production, so that the "economic" (even in its expanded sense implied here) contains mutually interdependent, dialectically interacting productionist and consumptionist sectors, with corresponding productionist and consumptionist ideologies. One of the most significant facts about contemporary society is that while these two realms are interdependent, an increasing degree of contradiction between them is developing, especially as consumptionism becomes the far more powerful ideology and its values begin to invade even the most classically productionist institutions. Thus, the famed "revolt against work." Yet one should not rashly conclude that one has discovered fatal contradictions in the system, especially when these depend on largely unconscious and instinctive activity. The consumptionist desire for gratification does not necessarily lead to a rejection of alienated labor, merely displeasure with it. Most good consumers recognize that they must (so they think) subject themselves to mindless toil, if they are to consume at a satisfactory level. Perhaps what is undermined most by consumptionism is not the capacity to engage in meaningless labor, but rather the capacity to engage in meaningful labor. Once intrinsic goodness is drained from production, only enforced labor is possible. The consumer submits him or herself to more or less regimented work out of a necessity for "survival" (i.e., survival as a commodity consumer, rather than existence in any other mode of being). Beyond this, only the passivity of consumption is conceivable. When called upon for more creative activity (voluntary association, political activism, etc.) the alibi is that all one's "energy" is wasted in the pursuit of "survival," when, in fact, it is one's imagination that is depleted.

conceded even a single grudging footnote to Orwell's magnificent political classic *Homage to Catalonia*. But now the word "Orwell" will be immortalized in thousands of résumés.

In the real world, the exploitation is even more blatant. According to John Hurt, star of the latest film version of *1984*, "We're moving closer to what it describes." His evidence for this momentous conclusion is far from astounding. "Look," he says, "at the bickering between East and West." (N.B.—in the book, the Superpowers were in a state of constant war, so why not subsume everything from propaganda wars to Blitzkrieg under the general rubric of "bickering"). It matters little whether we are overwhelmed by this *tour de force* of historical analysis. The point is: Talk Orwell. Talk *1984*. Talk Big Brother.

As Hurt remarks acutely, "Orwell is a hot topic."

Needless to say, advertising itself has not failed to make use of "1984" themes in order to sell products and to promote the ideology of free choice (for as we were told as early as 1970 by Toffler in *Future Shock*, the problem today is not lack of choice, but rather the dilemmas of "overchoice" in the affluent society).

An exquisite example of "1984" marketing comes from "United Technologies," who tell us that "Orwell was wrong about technology. Technology has not enslaved us. It has freed us." Orwell overlooked technological progress—in particular, the fact that large, expensive computers would give way to small, accessible machines. He knew nothing of The Chip, which has "made the computer so widespread" that it "removes the fears coming from Orwell's belief that the power of the computer would rest exclusively in the hands of an elite few."

Readers of the book will notice that this is a "belief" of which the "believer" himself was not aware. For in *1984*, information was concentrated not in computers, or in anything computer-like, but rather in "vast repositories where the corrected documents were stored." Yet, Orwell must hold this "belief" about computers, since the point of the ad is to show that he was wrong. "The electronic chip has put the power of the computer at the fingertips of anyone who wants to expand the scope and clarity of his thinking."

What is suppressed in this paean to the machine is the vast dimension of unfreedom entailed in such technological development: the workers who must adapt to the computer whatever their "wants" or desires, and no matter how much it routinizes their labor; the students who are compelled to learn to use it by the dictates of school authorities; the unconsciously chosen effects of the technology in reducing the "scope and clarity of thinking." Perhaps above all, this technology threatens autonomy by incorporating people into the technological system as information consumers (and very few are information creators!). Like Orwell's telescreen, the computer cannot be an effective means of control to the extent that it is monopolized by a few. The "network" must cast its net as broadly as possible in order to maximize integration into the system.

"United Technologies" indeed!

An even more blatant exploitation of the "1984" theme is Apple Computers' celebrated ad. In this brief but evocative drama, masses of zombies sit hypnotized before a giant telescreen, immobilized by the dominating image of Big Brother. Suddenly a woman rushes down the center aisle brandishing a sledgehammer. In a spectacular Olympian gesture of anti-authoritarianism she hurls the hammer across the hall and smashes the screen. The message: We are out of the grip of Big Brother . . . "Apple Computers."

But why "Apple Computers?" A translation for the literal minded. The "big names," like IBM, stand for big power, for manipulation and control. The Apple stands for the little guy, for "small is beautiful," for individual freedom. The images of Big Brother and the rebelling individual are thus appropriate. They represent the small and independent entrepreneur against the corporate giant, and personalized technology in opposition to totalitarian megamachines. Whether the company is really more David-than-Goliath-like, whether the machines are really warm and cuddly, is irrelevant. We are given two good symbolic reasons to buy an Apple.

Other symbolic connections are, however, to be avoided. While United Technologies argues that the computer offers us new levels of knowledge, we are presumably not to associate the bite of the Apple with Original Sin and the Fall from Paradise, an event occasioned by a similar promise.

"Who Needs The Thought Police?" Or "'What's On Tonight?"

Oceania, the society of *1984* is, in a sense, the direct antithesis of the consumer society of today. It is a society of material scarcity that maintains this condition, not through the ceaseless expansion of demands and desires, but through the planned limitation of supply.

The populace is kept dependent by the necessity of abject reliance on the State for basic necessities, and either through the perpetual maintenance of a condition of terror (in the case of the Outer Party), or one of ignorance and disorganization (in the case of the proles). The unsophisticated nature of its social conditioning makes it not surprising that the State would have to resort to terror to maintain order among the party members. And considering the abysmal standard of living provided to the second-class elite, one suspects that it is not only our hero, Winston, but most of his co-workers who also yearn to slit B. B.'s throat.

The ineptness of the rulers is illustrated best by their naive use of the telescreen. It serves primarily as a means of surveillance. While people do watch it, they are controlled not so much by their obsessive attachment to it as by their fear that it is constantly watching them. The big hit of every season is "The Hate," a repetitive miniseries which momentarily arouses malevolent passions in this passionless society. The State seems never to have discovered the potential of electronic media for control through positive feelings of attachment and dependence. In fact, the proles, who correspond most closely to the masses of today, are not even required to possess telescreens. As "Mr. Charrington" is able to comment, "I never had one of those things. Too expensive."

B. B., you blew it! The proles definitely revolted in 1985. No doubt they got pissed off after a bad football match, rampaged through the streets, and slaughtered the entire Inner Party so they could drink wine, not vile Victory Gin, for one delirious night.

In 1984, control is much more effective. The typical American family exercises its freedom of choice by watching over seven hours of television per day, as of 1983. While it took 15 years for viewing to increase from five to six hours, the next increment of an hour took but 11 years. If viewing continues to accelerate at this rate, it will reach 24 hours per day well before the middle of the next century, causing difficulties for other popular activities, like working and shopping.

So effectively have TV images invaded the collective consciousness that characters take on a supernatural, paradigmatic quality. While children were once named after favorite saints, admired historical figures, or beloved relatives, the preferred models are now soap-opera stars. The naming of children has always been a revealing ritual in every culture, showing the society's most deeply held values and aspirations. By the late 20th Century, parents' greatest desire was for their daughters to partake of the essential qualities of "Heather" and "Monica" of "General Hospital," and "Tara" of "All My Children."

Media images expand their dominance into every sphere of existence, as the culture of consumption generates a morbid dialectic of dehumanization. On the one hand, it drains life from organic culture and from the person by its substitution of prefabricated images for elaborated forms of life. It creates as the end of all its manipulations a spectral non-person, an *Untermensch* of pure externality, a being defined by images and "life style." On the other hand, it appropriates this very being in its perfection and presents it to the consumer as an idealized image of the present.

Examples of such media heroes are abundant—their number is legion. Perhaps the most appealingly grotesque is rock star Billy Idol. As his name indicates, he is a demigod, both man (the mundane "Billy") and deity (object of worship—"Idol"), thus allowing both identification with a personality and proper awe in the face of the spectacular. As usual, the imagination reveals more than reason intends, for everyone (presumably even rock fans) knows that an idol is a false god. Thus the manifest intention of the ritual is both to worship and to identify with the false. Even more obvious is the significance of "idol" as "image." There is an ironic progression from the human ("Billy") to its negation by the pure image ("Idol").

The content of the image is no less revealing, for we find in Mr. Idol's presentations a vision of violence, necrophilia, and total alienation. In his video "Dancing With Myself," our hero is left alone in a completely solipsistic world. The only other semi-human images presented are hordes of mangled, decaying creatures attempting to invade his (presumably post-holocaust) citadel, and the silhouette (even more radically diminished image) of a naked, chained woman. In "White Wedding" he brutally forces a wedding ring onto his bride's finger, causing her to bleed. Not surprisingly, Mr. Idol has been attacked for his demeaning depiction of women in his pursuit of striking images. His response to criticism is that his intention is merely to *depict* the exploitation of women, rather than actually to exploit women. But since "depictions" can obviously be complicit in exploitation, this is a very bad argument. Of course, Mr. Idol might claim that he was merely *depicting* a bad argument.

While it is the modus operandi of electronic media to commodify culture, the music video is perhaps the genre which is most advanced in perfecting this process. All values—social, political, moral, or spiritual—are a suitable resource for the creation of stylized images and superficial themes. What was once done with perhaps greatest sophistication in fashion photography is now accomplished with vastly expanded impact on consciousness in videos. Several have recently taken up the theme of "revolution." China is a popular subject matter, since it offers the powerful image of flowing red flags and exotic characters. The choicest travesty is, however, Duran-Duran's "New Moon on Monday," which takes place in some Communist-looking mystery country. The singers parade around as revolutionaries against the authoritarian state, giving out leaflets, carrying torches, and singing incomprehensible but no doubt profoundly symbolic lyrics. The authorities call out the troops, but these menacing characters are so intimidated by the growing "movement" that they scatter without a fight. One Duran seems more confused than the next by the entire chain of events. But what matter? The song is a super-hit and the revolution doesn't need coherence in order to be an effective choreographic backdrop.

What Is "Truth"?

One of Orwell's most powerful insights is his understanding of the breakdown of the concept of objective truth. It would have been entirely natural to present the leaders of the Inner Party as ideological fanatics who are unconditionally committed to their beliefs and prejudices. By avoiding this option, he made it possible to present them as much more authentic representatives of modern nihilism (and, as Nietzsche pointed out, the modern State is one of history's preeminent expressions of nihilistic will to power). They exhibit in its most extreme form the decomposition of all ideals of truth, justice, and goodness. As O'Brien states, "Reality exists in the human mind and nowhere else." Accordingly, "nothing exists except through human consciousness." All barriers to triumphant subjectivity are eliminated. The ego can assert itself without moral or metaphysical limitation.

The abolition of objective truth, especially as manifested in objective value, is a premise not only of the authoritarian society in which might makes right, but also of the consumerist society, in which the image must always be right. The only "objective" world becomes the world of "facts," of "brute matter" and of "brute force," and the world of the processes of production and material transformation—the realm of "necessity," as it has been called. Meaning and value reside in an entirely different sphere, the realm of the relative and subjective. Subjectivity is thus banished from nature, and objectivity from the human spirit.

But objective value does not truly disappear. Rather, it is retained in a completely alienated form. For the sphere of production includes not only mere material objects, but also commodity-images imbued with intensely experienced value. In so far as these images take on the illusion of objective reality and gain power over the subject, objective value remains in existence, but in an entirely opaque, mystified form. The fetishism of commodities thereby permits the simultaneous disintegration of authentic objective values and domination by illusory objective values.

The Land Of Spam

If one were pressed to find a single image for the society of commodity consumption, perhaps the most felicitous choice would be Spam. Spam succeeds in embodying at once the productionist power of material transformation and the consumptionist power of imagination. It is the ultimate symbol of the transformation of natural substance and sensuous qualities into a thoroughly artificial material with an entirely fabricated image. So complete has been its metamorphosis that consumers surveyed have difficulty speculating as to its makeup. No one really knows what it is. It is the closest thing to generic "food," and might easily be taken to be the *materia prima* of the entire universe. As Thales (not to be confused with any computer language THALES) might say, "All is Spam."

Yet it is, in fact, real animal protoplasm that has been transformed into the commodity "Spam." But while Spam arose from the destruction of living animals, it has in turn itself generated its own non-living animal image, "The Spam Animal." This is an image created by the Hormel Company to be loved by consumers, who can then transfer their affection to the product itself. Unfortunately, however, dangers lurk in this seemingly innocuous concept. For as a company executive noted, "If we put too much emphasis on the Spam animal, people will be afraid that we kill it and put it in the can."

Interestingly, there is no anxiety about the possibility that Hormel Co. might be killing actual, real-world animals to put them in cans. For

The materia prima of the entire universe?

Stephen Duplantier

not being familiar commodities, these creatures have no place in the consumptionist universe. (Urban children grow up unaware of the fact that meat comes from animals, rather than factories, and the truth never really sinks in).

In the Free Market of Ideas one is not likely to hear a "message" like "Mommy, can I have another glob of reconstituted pigflesh?" "Why, of course, Jason, dear, and wash it down with a big glass of Kemical Kola!" No, the only realistic fear in such a world is that the poor imaginary Spam animal might be put back into the very product that generated it (sent like a Spam to the slaughter, as it were).

But the dialectic of delusion moves one brilliant step forward. Our executive asks, "Remember the 'Pet Rock?'" Of course, we remember, but, if not, we can always be reminded, for in the universe of images nothing is ever lost. In *1984*, the past was obliterated. In 1984 everything goes into the memory banks, since all is potential capital.

The Pet Rock was a pet that was not a pet. Its development is instructive. First moment: Irony of a thing lacking all the qualities that make it what it is. Latent signification: the inorganic quality of our world—a petrified pet for plastic people. Second moment: Humor of treating a rock like a pet. The rough edges of this rock are rounded off, and absurdity domesticated as a conversation piece. Third moment: Herd-Instinct, as the good consumer acquires whatever is seen or talked about. A new contribution to the Gross National Garbage.

How can some elements of this classic fad be recycled for the greater glory of Spam? "We will create a cage for the Spam Animal!" suggests our creative marketing executive. The cage will, of course, be empty. The logic is unimpeachable: If the Spam Animal is not in the cage, it cannot be thought of as being slaughtered and put in the can. One can thus safely express one's allegiance to Spam (show product loyalty) by exhibiting in one's home the *absence* of the imaginary Spam animal.

Lest anyone doubt the persistence of Mind in the land of images, this quadruple negation (which puts to shame the pitiable double negations of ancient dialecticians) is one that can be comprehended by any child today. While it is true that some types of rationality atrophy in consumer society, it is equally true that others flourish extravagantly.

No Orwellian world, this! When confronted with the cage for the non-animal, the Orwellian newspeaker would be speechless, or at best might mutter "Where's the animal?" Today's newthinker recognizes immediately that the cage is not designed for animals.

Sex In The Ruins

In Oceania, a traditional productionist view of sexuality and
reproduction prevails, at least for the party members. Sex is solely
for the production of offspring, and is assimilated into the sphere of
duty to the State. Desire and pleasure are stigmatized as subversive of
the regimentation on which the system depends. Sexual repression
performs the important function of capturing instinctual energy, which
can then be channeled into authoritarian political hysteria. The process
roughly follows Reich's analysis in *The Mass Psychology of Fascism*. In
view of the political nature of repression, desired sexual activity becomes
an act of rebellion against the State.

The limitations of this theory of repression and its negation were long
ago demonstrated in Marcuse's analysis of repressive desublimation. If
sexual expression can be redirected according to the requirements of
commodity consumption, sexuality can be effectively neutralized as a
subversive force. This is what has, in fact, occurred in contemporary
consumptionist society, though to a degree unimagined in Marcuse's
problematic. Such a solution is hinted at by Orwell, insofar as the proles
are controlled in part by the availability of pornography, prostitution, etc.
Yet it is not clear precisely how these controls operate. Presumably, they
perform an entirely negative function—draining off instinctual energy,
rather than manipulating it politically. But the possibility of using

Détournement by Stephen Duplantier

"The Objet a *is ultimately nothing but a certain curvature of the space itself."*
—Pamela Anderson

the instincts to integrate the populace into the system of power more perfectly is hardly explored.

In the society of consumption, on the other hand, no resource is left unexploited in the pursuit of capital accumulation. Businessmen can charge the services of prostitutes to their Visa or MasterCard, customers of sexually explicit telephone messages are billed automatically, swingers magazines can cater profitably to a lower-middle class Republican clientele, and Playboy, Penthouse and their ilk have long been established as respectable Big Business.

On the level of the individual, there is also an imperative demanding the exploitation of sexuality. "Sex appeal" is essential for the successful marketing of one's personality, "image," and "successful life style." In the world of commodities, the "self" becomes highly valued capital. Accumulation of sex appeal requires investment in health clubs, exercise equipment, Jane Fonda workout books, plastic surgery, cosmetics, and a variety of sports and diet doctors. In *1984*, Winston looked around the canteen of the Ministry of Truth, and was shocked that everyone was so ugly. In 1984, the society of consumption requires beautiful people. To project the correct image, one must possess the right "assets"—calculable in quantities of calf, biceps, thigh, waist, etc. And having developed these qualities, the good consumer can then buy some "designer band-aids" (only "three for 99 cents!"). These ingenious commodities are designed not to "aid" in healing cuts and scratches, but rather to "aid" in drawing attention to one's most well-developed body parts. The Body Politic may be sick, but the Body Economic thrives!

Crimes Against Nurture

In the authoritarian society of *1984*, the production of children is an obligation to the State, and youth are subjected to rigid discipline and control (membership in the "Spies," for example). In the consumptionist society the very production of offspring conflicts increasingly with the "independent life-style" (read: complete dependence on maximized commodity consumption) that is the ideal self-image. The result is a decline in the birth rate, except among the most backward and uneducated, and a tendency to "warehouse" both the very young and the very old in the most efficient, cost-effective manner, resulting in minimal interference with productive and consumptive activity.

The long-term effects of the consignment of young children to commercial day-care centers can only be speculated upon. Presumably, the displacement of much of early-childhood experience from the family to a more depersonalized milieu will have far-reaching implications for the evolution of character-structure. While the decline of the intense relationships of the nuclear family may signal the obsolescence of the patriarchal, authoritarian conditioning excoriated by Reich, it may also mean the decomposition of the developed, complex personality which flowered (however faded the flower may often have been) in the bourgeois epoch.

A certain insight into the consumptionist imagination can be gained from the widely publicized McMartin Preschool child abuse case in Southern California (the Oasis of the Bizarre) in which over one hundred children were allegedly molested by their caretakers over a period of years. The children were reportedly abused in multifarious ways, including being sodomized and filmed in pornographic films. Presumably, having exhausted the means of exploiting the children on the premises, the ingenious entrepreneurs offered their adult clients kiddies-to-go, taking the children to "health clubs" for the sexual use of customers. The parents of the children involved for years had no suspicion that any such activities took place. When allegations began to emerge, some parents noted that they had been asked not to visit the center during the day. Soon, there was a general consensus that abuse was rampant, and child after child began to reveal the sordid details.

The problem was, as we later discovered, that none of it had really happened, and that the whole affair was a product of paranoid suspicions and mass delusion. Yet, the case is revealing in that it shows what seems possible in a consumptionist universe. The delusion was an extrapolation of consumptionist values: the imaginary McMartin Preschool, infinitely more real than the actual one, is an enterprise that can serve as the model of the capitalist virtue of maximum exploitation of resources. First, it permits the parents to carry on their functions as commodity-producers and consumers, unhampered by the familial demands—in this it is like capitalist child-care in general. Second, it allows young children to begin their lives as commodity consumers by using day-care services—again this is increasingly the norm. But, third, it is innovative in allowing young children to be recycled as sexual commodities even as they consume and they free their parents to produce and consume more, thus achieving a triple contribution to the GNP.

Politics, The Opiate Of The Masses, Or, Hart Of A Heartless World

In Oceania, politics was abolished. In the consumer society, politics as authentic participation in civic life is virtually non-existent. Yet, the political is retained as an important element of the legitimation process. While the public has long had a dim awareness of the nature of the game, and cynicism continually erodes whatever political faith persists, people still cling tenuously to some remnants of the political illusion.

While the masses' true loyalty is to the commodity and not to the political system, every four years the American State—much like its counterparts elsewhere—takes a new stab at mending its fractured legitimacy. The means, needless to say, is the marketing of a fresh crop of politicians as new, improved commodities. One of the most noteworthy Grade A products offered to the political consumer was Senator Gary Hart. Sen. Hart attempted to recycle several aspects of the JFK image with moderate success mystique-wise. What is less known is his excellent pedigree of generations of image-consciousness. The Senator's surname originally derived from the family name "Eberhart Penz." This alien, Germanic patronymic was wisely Americanized into the more acceptable "Hartpence." But this was still a somewhat unusual denomination. It remained for Senator Gary himself to take the decisive third step, reducing it to "Hart," a name evoking both a noble beast and the seat of all benevolence within the human person.

It is fitting that someone possessing such originality should base his appeal above all on his commitment to "new ideas." Sen. Hart assured the public that he had "new ideas," and many Hart fans indeed reported that they supported him precisely because of these very "new ideas." His opponents (especially Mr. Mondale, who represented "the traditional Democratic coalition," an old, worn-out, but occasionally useful idea) did not fail to point out that even while proclaiming these "new ideas," Hart had failed to reveal their precise content, or to explain in what sense they were "new." Yet, this only showed the hopeless confusion of these old-fashioned politicians concerning the current state of the electoral process. Sen. Hart's term "new ideas" signified in no way that he actually possessed *specific concepts* in his *mind* that were in some way *novel*. Rather, the term signified that he was to have the image of "a person having new ideas"—the question of the existence some ideas or other is at best irrelevant. In fact, the disclosure of truly innovative concepts might have made the candidate threatening to large segments of the populace, and would certainly have complicated and hindered the process of selling him as a generally consumable product.

Do Images Have Standing?

As political institutions are ever more perfectly absorbed into the spectacle of commodity-consumption, "justice" has its turn to become a media commodity. While courtroom drama has been a media staple since Perry Mason, the exploitation of this theme reached new heights with the introduction of authentic courtroom testimony in the New Bedford "Barroom Gang-Rape Trial." Cable News Network, which presented hour after hour of detailed testimony concerning the rape, solemnly defended its decision to do so, on grounds that it was important to inform the public about this crucial issue. In other words, CNN will present anything, no matter how squalid, lurid or offensive, no matter how positive the effect on ratings, so long as it promotes the cause of Good Citizenship.

This profaning of the sacred judiciary did not go uncriticized, albeit confusedly. A professor from the prestigious Annenberg School of Communications proclaimed such phenomena "show trials," and likened them to practices in Stalinist Russia, China, and Iran. Yet, this particular Orwellian allusion is misplaced, for the traditional authoritarian function of the cases mentioned is confounded with the consumptionist function of media trials today. The professor confuses the "show trial" of the past with the "trial show" of today.

If TV trials present us with the image of justice, we are now faced with the even stranger possibility of justice for images. Images have become so central to contemporary society that they may soon earn entitlement to protection by the judicial system. The image raising this question is found at the "Cadillac Ranch" in Texas, where ten Cadillacs are buried in a vertical position with their tailfins protruding into the air. The three creators of this valuable image have sued the Hard Rock Café of Hollywood, California, for $1.5 million for having a 1959 Cadillac protruding from the Café's roof. The heinous crime committed by the Café operators is "image appropriation," a serious offense in a world in which images are among the most highly valued properties.

Image-rustlers beware! The folks from the Ranch will give you your comeuppance.

Decadence Hits Workers' Paradise

While consumptionist values are firmly established in Western societies, they increasingly infect the "Eastern bloc" also as production continues to climb and Western influences maintain their slow but continuous process of infiltration. Symbolic of this historic tendency is the introduction of high fashion modeling in Moscow. Recently, the elite of the State capitalist regime sat back and enjoyed their Vodka Colas, as they were treated to the same parade of ghostly figures that one is accustomed to seeing in New York, Paris, or Milan. While the models went through the same mechanical posturing as do their Western counterparts, the themes differed somewhat. While in New York one can see expensive caricatures of, for example, the Ecuadoran peasant, the Astronaut, or (irony of ironies!) the Bag Lady, the Muscovites were served their own unique brand of cultural vampirism. The big hit of the show followed a Socialist theme: not Proletarian Realism, however, but rather stylish, and highly stylized outfits based on the Great October Revolution. While it is no secret that the Revolution has long been dead in Russia, such an event indicates a surprising degree of ideological disintegration, and suggests unexpected advancement toward the general substitution of consumptionist values for authoritarian ones.

The People's Republic of China has been no more successful in preventing the return of the repressed commodity. It is no secret that the post-Mao regime is making a concerted effort to incorporate into the socialist system all the advances of Western technological society. Presumably "economics in command" will lead to rapid commodification of the culture. Already the State has begun to build luxury condominiums near Hong Kong, so that rich capitalist executives can commute between the People's Republic and the sweatshops in which they oppress the toiling masses. While this apparent sin against socialist morality can no doubt be explained away in the name of the exigencies of socialist development, the true and mortal sin is the spectacle of the "beautiful people" living the "good life."

Another force destined to transform China is the invasion by Western tourists. The People's Republic is now investing in tourism in a big, and often ingenious, way. For example, there are two kinds of hotels offered to the Western visitor. One is typified by a newly-built structure we might call the "Running Dog Hilton." A Western-style high-rise luxury hostelry, it is topped by that pinnacle of sophisticated elegance, the revolving lounge. So awe-stricken are the Chinese by this magnificent edifice, that they photograph themselves with it as a background at all hours of the day.

At the other extreme of tourist accommodations is a complex we might call the "Immiseration Inn," a remodeled commune with just enough comforts of home to make the atmosphere exotic rather than oppressive. Here the visitor can play peasant, inhabiting homely dwellings, taking the oxen for an occasional spin, and even doing a Marie-Antoinette-like stint in the rice paddies.

Longchamp advertisement

Longchamps Bags. Fabriqué en Chine

Even more menacing to the remnants of socialist ideology is the growing interest of Chinese leaders in advertising. As two American advertising executives recently testified: "They want to believe in advertising." And, indeed, they should, since twenty-five years after the Revolution it would be naive to think that a billion people could be kept under control by reciting the various inanities of Mao's *Little Red Book* (Little-Read Book?). True, the Socialist Leaders still had reservations about the quintessential capitalist techniques of marketing, but their misgivings were rapidly laid to rest. As the executives reported: "They asked us, 'Does advertising lie?' We had great answers and the Chinese accepted them!"

Presumably, elites East and West have found common ground: the truth is what works.

The Sick Society

In Oceania, "there were fear, hatred, and pain, but not dignity of emotion, no deep or complex sorrows." Today, we find a similar loss of complexity of feeling, but with it a loss of the intensity of feeling that was retained even in Orwell's dystopia. Instead of fear, hatred, and pain, we increasingly encounter anxiety, annoyance, and malaise. Life is perceived as a burden, but not because of the oppressiveness or injustice of our mode of existence. Rather, the "cost of living" seems too high. "The bottom line" is slightly in the red.

Strangely, as "lifestyle" flourishes, life increasingly has less meaning. An epidemic of suicide has broken out, for example, among teenagers, the vanguard of the consumer society. The rate of suicide among the young has increased 50% in only a decade. Especially in suburbia, the most advanced sector of contemporary society, shocking outbreaks appear. In a single Dallas, Texas, suburb, seven teenagers killed themselves in a single year. In a northern California suburb, the total reached twelve. In one case, a child allegedly chose this path as the result of severe depression following the news that he would have to wear braces for several years. Non-existence was apparently preferable to the projection of an incorrect image. Whether this report is accurate or not, there is certainly a severe crisis resulting from the growth of narcissistic personality structures. Increasing numbers of people are unable to plan for, or even conceive of, a meaningful future that is worth struggling for, and become locked in an eternal present of passive, uncreative consumption.

Much in line with the proliferation of such problems, one popular model of the contemporary world depicts it as "the therapeutic society." This concept contains a partial truth, for many institutions have been transformed according to the therapeutic perspective, specializing in "treatment" of the "maladjusted." This is just one aspect of a generalized trend. As society progressively disintegrates into a collection of atomized, egoistic consumers, every element of the alienated personality spawns hordes of therapeutic experts inundating the public with manuals, guides, tapes, videos, courses, groups, sessions, etc. All becomes technique. As a "sleep expert" was recently asked by a television interviewer, "Should we regard sleep as a natural function, or as a skill to be learned?" One may indeed wonder.

Yet all is not therapy, and the model in question is a flawed one.

Therapy is just one, albeit pervasive, aspect of the consumptionist and productionist sectors. It is another commodity aimed at satisfying the ever-expanding needs and desires generated by consumer society. Just as every organ, tissue, and even cell of the body must ultimately be exploited by the medical industry, so every dark recess of the psyche must ultimately be exploited by the therapy business. And to the degree that we produce alienated, but at the same time narcissistic and self-indulgent consumers, we create the ideal customers for this growth industry.[2]

The End of History

Perhaps the most striking similarity between the society of *1984* and the society of consumption is in the striving of both to eliminate history. In *1984*, "history has stopped. Nothing exists except an endless present in which the Party is always right." In 1984, history is indeed coming to an end. This is the imminent fate of Western society and the eventual fate of all that comes under its suzerainty. Beginning with the secularization of the Judeo-Christian eschatological vision, the West has been an historical civilization. Historical time has been the framework in which human destiny has worked itself out, whether this destiny has been conceived of as the conversion of all nations to Christianity, the triumph of civilization over savagery and barbarism, or the establishment of universal Communism.

This historical movement is now being definitively terminated by the expansion of Capital to its limits. There is now a consensus in the "developed" world that material production and commodity consumption are the fundamental tasks of humanity (the ultimate "bottom line"). Consequently, there are for the "advanced" societies no transcendent or ideal standards by which to judge historical movement or even the value of particular forms of life. We are left to wait for the dawning realization that under the mask of "economic growth" hides an eternal recurrence of the same. We begin to fall into a new cyclical time lacking the mythic dimension of primitive temporality. We are left in an "endless present" in which not the Party but the Commodity is always right. If we can't take it, there is always therapy.

---

2. While psychotherapy will no doubt continue to perform its assigned function in the system of production and consumption, there have been valiant attempts to uphold the ideal of critical and radical psychoanalysis. For the most notable and most incisive of these, see Joel Kovel, *The Age of Desire: Reflections of a Radical Psychoanalyst* (New York: Pantheon Books, 1981).

The End Of Humanity?

Perhaps it is not only history, but humanity itself, that is now dispensable. Presumably, as the self becomes more and more shadowy in a world of images, we can eventually disappear completely. The technology is, in any case, ready to step into the breach. One can imagine the home of the not too distant future. The reassuring sound of the television drones on, as all the best programs are faithfully recorded on the VCR machine. The computer terminal is on-line, bringing in all the latest news, in addition to information about sales and specials at leading department stores. Our user-friendly computer is programmed to order key products automatically at pre-selected prices, and to print-out news items of special interest. The telephone answering machine is always alert, repeating its witty message concerning no one being at home, and taping all the prerecorded calls that increasingly bombard it. All the dials are set, so the washing-machine washes our clothes and the automatic dryer dries them, while the oven—better yet, the radar range—cooks to calculated perfection our pre-packaged, processed and prepared food products. It is, of course, a self-cleaning oven. All the while, the digital clock pulsates facelessly onward.

The End Of Thinking?

In *1984*, Newspeak was created to narrow the range of thought, through a continual process of simplification and elimination of vocabulary. Today, the range of thought has not so much been narrowed as rechanneled. The language expands regularly, above all with technical vocabulary and terminology needed to keep pace with the process of commodity-production. On the other hand, modes of thought and expression at variance with the requirements of technological and consumptionist society begin to disappear. For example, mass-media and the educational system work to dissolve local and cultural diversity, which produce unnecessary conflict with the dominant productionist and consumptionist values. There has thus been a process of homogenization and standardization of thought and language, while at the same time a huge expansion and diversification has taken place within the narrowed limits.

The psychology of belief has changed accordingly. Orwell's Doublethink required a certain quantity of mental discipline, since one was obliged to hold two contradictory opinions which one knew to be in conflict. Such clarity and willfulness worthy of a Tertullian no longer exists today. While people are expected to accept ideological principles, they are seldom aware of any conflicts between various articles of faith, or between these and other areas of experience. A vague and confused adherence to amorphous beliefs is all that is expected. Furthermore, as the "information society" overwhelms the mind with an endless clutter of disconnected and unanalyzed data, the chance of any particular belief or combination of them becoming a threat to the order of things is increasingly less likely.

The Enduring Relevance Of 1984

Having said much about the ways in which *1984* does *not* describe contemporary Western society, I feel compelled to add a few final words concerning the profundity and relevance of the work. My final reference to the book will therefore be to the passage that I believe to be its most brilliant. Near the end of the narrative, O'Brien comments that it is clear enough to everyone *how* the Party rules, but that the more significant and challenging question is *why*. He poses this question to Winston: "Why should we want power?" Winston replies that "You are ruling for our own good . . . . You believe that human beings are not fit to govern themselves, and therefore—," at which point he is administered an excruciatingly intense shock for having given such a ridiculous answer.

As O'Brien explains, "The Party seeks power entirely for its own sake." What is desired is not merely any kind of power, but "pure power." A contradiction is encountered in the individual's search for power, for the quest is doomed to end in failure. All human beings will weaken, die, decay. The entire undertaking therefore seems futile. But if one can "make complete, utter subjugation, if he can escape from his identity, if her can merge himself in the Party so that he is the Party, then he is all-powerful and immortal." Power can once more have meaning, especially insofar as its truest form is attained—not mere power over matter, "but, above all, over the mind."

Orwell thus gives us a perceptive insight into the psychology of authoritarianism, but even more importantly, he touches on some universal aspects of modern humanity. Indeed, he is hinting at some essential qualities of civilization itself. For if, in authoritarian society, the elite are driven by the quest for a power which raises them above their limitations and mortality, this is no more than the striving that is identical with the history of civilization. It is equally the Truth of the society of consumption. The commodities that become the *raison d'être* of the person as consumer are not mere objects, but images also. The consumer does not only buy a collection of products, but also a constellation of commodity-images constituting an imagined self. While society is rather frank in admitting that to be successful one must "sell oneself," it has been less explicit in stating the corollary: that one must also *buy oneself.*

Yet everyone knows that this is true. In consumer society, one does not have to dominate in the style of an authoritarian elite in order to exercise significant power. Instead, one may invest in the production of the correct self-image and successfully sell it to others. Given the multitude of levels of status within the pyramidal techno-bureaucratic system and within the labyrinthine hierarchy of commodities, one has enormous possibilities for relative success or failure in image-credibility. The promise of the society is, though, that to the extent that one succeeds in this endeavor, one rises above mundane existence—"everydayness"— and achieves a kind of idealized Being. Consequently, it is possible to escape, however precariously, from mortality and the limitations of the actually existing self. The entire project is fraudulent, but it is no more fraudulent than the identification of the self with the authoritarian State or Party that Orwell describes. In both cases, there is a denial of reality in the pursuit of recognition by self and others—the pursuit of "power over mind."

The End Of Civilization

Our theme has been the dominant position of consumptionism in contemporary advanced capitalist society. While Big Brother stands in the wings, ever ready to apply the electrodes, at center stage in today's Spectacle of Power is our *Giant Economy-Size Brother. The Commodity.* There is a danger that one might infer that since ideological control is so powerful today, there is even less opportunity for escape from our Brother than from Orwell's. This is not necessarily the case.

First, it must be recognized that consumptionism has, in fact, challenged the traditional authoritarian structure of society. To the extent that productionist society in its classical period labored under the yoke of the Performance Principle, we have gained a degree of freedom with the deterioration of this principle. Thus far, the consequences of this freedom have been deeply disturbing, linked as they have been to the dissolution of the organic fabric of society. As Janis Joplin so aptly pointed out, freedom can be "just another word for nothing left to lose."

Yet, there are two moments in the development of contemporary culture, and the fulfillment of each is a real historical possibility. On the one hand, there is the obsessive consumption that has been described here, an endless striving toward an elusive fulfillment, the progressive destruction of all existing values in the name of a dream that is incapable of definition, though it is endlessly defined and redefined in a million ways, by the world of consumption. Of course, this quest is doomed to failure. It can only lead to a spiritual immiseration less bearable than the material immiseration of the early industrial era. The true crisis of capitalism (in both its corporate and statist varieties) is a crisis of the spirit.

The impasse confronting consumptionism creates hope that the way will open for the unfolding of another moment of consumptionist society—the submerged utopian moment whose fate lies with the radical imagination. To the extent that the imagination has unbound itself from its subservience to the commodity, it has engendered a vision of completeness, happiness, fulfillment, self-realization, and reconciliation. It is a vision in which we are lost neither in the domineering one nor the nihilistic many. With the dissolution of the authoritarian structure of productionist society, civilized humanity can for the first time begin again to dream the dream of wholeness—or, to speak more accurately, allow that dream to make its way into our common consciousness.

The fate of this vision rests with our success in reconciling imagination with theoretical and practical reason, that is, with a new understanding of humanity and nature, and a new practice of liberatory social transformation. If this can be achieved, then, when the dialectic of civilization has finally played itself out, disinherited humanity may finally awaken to the abyss in which it has been falling. And, in the face of the void, it may then take up, in earnest and in jest, its impossible, inevitable quest for a plenitude of being.

Alchemical Sublimation. From Geber's Works, *London 1678.*

In the face of the void, disinherited humanity may then take up, in earnest and in jest, its impossible, inevitable quest for a plenitude of being."

The Macrocosm and the Microcosm from Robert Fludd's *Utriusque Cosmi, Maioris scilicet et Minoris, metaphysica, physica, atque technica Historia*, 1617

7
LAUGHING MATTERS, OR, IN PRAISE OF FOLLY

"Two dangers threaten the universe: order and disorder."[1]
—Paul Valéry

aul Valéry's aphorism seems like a sort of proto-Catch-22.
Whatever the intent, it plays on our fear that there's no possible
middle ground through which to pass safely. Either we're crushed
by the repressive forces of order or lost in meaningless, nihilistic chaos.
But don't panic (about this anyway). There is indeed a way to negotiate
a path between Valéry's twin oppressors, the suffocating Scylla and the
convulsive Charybdis.

It is the way of laughter. Not the titter or the giggle. The real laugh.
The laugh of the Real. Above all, it is through the howling, Boschian
belly laugh, the laugh that delights in the vital, the creative, and the
spontaneous. It affirms these inexorable realities in the face of the
annihilating powers of stifling orderliness or deadly disorder. It's in their
faces.

In fact, we human beings have always expressed our deepest truths,
our most deeply disturbing insights, in a spirit of comedy. There's
nothing more profoundly philosophical than the comedic. To attain the
deepest wisdom, we must learn to laugh deeply.

1. In "La Crise de l'Esprit" (1919); online at http://classiques.uqac.ca/classiques/Valery_
paul/crise_de_lesprit/valery_esprit.pdf.

Assemblage by Stephen Duplantier

Take the Revolution and Run

Traditional cultures have known this. As a result, they have always opened up a huge imaginary space in which the Trickster figure has appeared. Trickster has taken on many forms, ranging from the Fool in Medieval society to Coyote in Native American cultures. Tricksters have needed a large fantasy field because to do their job they need to run rampant. They have kept very busy reminding people not to take their myths, their rituals, their symbols, indeed, their traditions and culture itself, too seriously, and too literally.

Later, a European sage, Erasmus, argued that there is a Path of Folly that leads to wisdom. And he was right. But it turns out to be a more wayward path and a much crazier wisdom than even he imagined.

The best of humor arises from the clash between the official story about ourselves and the world, and the subversive, chaotic, revolutionizing, anarchic trauma of the Real. We sometimes call this Real "*sur*reality," for it always appears as *more real* than ordinary pale "reality." Such humor expresses the dialectic between boring, deadening everyday consciousness and what lies latent and hidden in the pre-conscious and the unconscious. The most hilarious (what some call the most "hysterical") humor juxtaposes what is conscious and what lies in the deepest levels of the unconscious. True humor is all about truth. It's all philosophy.

For example? Though often dismissed as mere ludic absurdism, Woody Allen's humor contains elements of the most profound mockery. There is a philosophical agenda. Often, his carefully chosen target is an abstract, idealist outlook that ignores the material realities of the human condition, or pretends that it can do so. For example, contemplating the idea of immortality, Allen comments, "If my soul exists without my body, I am convinced that all my clothes will be loose-fitting."[2] How many untold millions (even idealist philosophers) have had this feeling, without being able to pin it down so lucidly?

In his mock-existentialist piece "The Condemned," Allen mentions that his anti-hero Cloquet "hated reality, but realized that it was still the only place to get a good steak."[3] Later, he muses to himself, "Rely more on the body—the body is more dependable. It shows up for meetings, it looks good in a sports jacket, and where it really comes in handy is when you want to get a rubdown."[4] He observes that while in prison, Cloquet

---

2. Woody Allen, *The Complete Prose of Woody Allen* (New York: Random House, 1991), p. 10.
3. Ibid., p. 307.
4. Ibid, p. 310.

questioned the reality of death: "Men die, but does Cloquet die? This question puzzled him, but a few simple line drawings on a pad done by one of the guards set the whole thing clear."[5]

In "My Apology" Allen puts himself in the shoes (the sandals?) of Socrates, but continually makes ironic comments about the absurdity of the Platonic idealism that Socrates usually mouths. When his disciple Agathon mentions that Socrates/Allen had previously taught that death is like sleep, he replies, "Yes, but the difference is that when you're dead and somebody yells, 'Everybody up, its morning,' it's very hard to find your slippers."[6] Allen manages to convey concisely with ironic humor what the always witty and never quite humorous Nietzsche also sought to disclose: whatever fantastic ideas philosophers and other would-be escape artists may entertain, we all know that we actually *are* our bodies.

Sadly, contemporary American philosophy is the last place to look for enlightenment on our topic of humor. If, just for laughs, you were to check out the fairly numerous websites on philosophical humor, your hopes would quickly be dashed. The voluminous material found there consists mostly of nerdy attempts at hilarity, logic exercises masquerading as humor, and in-jokes about the profession (Q: How do you get a philosopher off your front porch? A: Pay for the pizza).

The universal favorite seems to be the one in which Descartes goes into a bar and one of his pals greets him with "Bonjour, Réné, how about a beer?" To which the philosopher replies, "I think not," and promptly disappears. Not bad, even if not so good, but you're more likely to find something even more cringe-provoking as this: "Aristotelian kiss—a kiss performed using techniques gained solely from theoretical speculation untainted by any experiential data by one who feels that the latter is irrelevant anyway." After which most readers will be ready to kiss off the topic of philosophical humor entirely.

Before giving up entirely, though, we should look at several recent books that touch on this topic. In *I Think, Therefore I Laugh*, philosophical mathematician John Allen Paulos claims that "conceptual humor and analytical philosophy resonate at a very deep level."[7] It's been said that the problem with science fiction is that it manages to be bad science and bad fiction all at the same time. Similarly, in Paulos's supposed marriage between philosophy and humor, it's a challenge to

---

5. Ibid. p. 312.
6. Ibid., p. 341.
7. John Allen Paulos, *I Think, Therefore I Laugh: The Flip Side of Philosophy* (New York: Columbia University Press, 2000), p. x.

find much that's either very philosophical or very humorous.

Poor Paulos just doesn't have an ear for the comedic. He's capable of including among his very limited collection of jokes the following clunker, though it's far from the least humorous in his collection. The effort has at least the virtue of brevity, if not that of wit: "George goes to the You-Bet-Your-Life computer dating service to register his requirements (axioms). He wants someone who is white, not very talkative, comfortable in fur, yet disdainful of city life. The computer sends him a polar bear."[8] Not only is this an utter groaner, but it leads nowhere philosophically. Paulos could at least have told us how he found out what bears think of cities.

Fortunately, Ted Cohen, who wrote *Jokes: Philosophical Thoughts on Joking Matters*,[9] has an excellent sense of humor. He's at his best when he analyzes Jewish humor and he offers hilarious examples of the ironic wit that comes out of that rich tradition. As he notes, the Jewish people have for thousands of years had an ironic relation to their societies. They have occupied the perilous position of being the outsiders on the inside. This has led them to develop an acute sense of irony as a means of coping with conditions of oppression and exclusion. As Cohen notes, "if your joke works, you will make people laugh at your oppressor, and if you are very lucky (and your joke is very good), you may even make your oppressor laugh at himself."[10] As Nietzsche made much the same point: "Not by wrath does one kill but by laughter."[11]

Here's one of the best of the jokes that Cohen recounts. It appears on his book's home page for all to see, so I don't have to feel excessively guilty about giving it away.

> *Abe and his friend Sol are out for a walk. . . . Passing a Christian church, they notice a curious sign in front that says "$1,000 to anyone who will convert." "I wonder what that's about," says Abe. "I think I'll go in and have a look. I'll be back in a minute; just wait for me." Sol sits on the sidewalk bench and waits patiently for nearly half an hour. Finally, Abe reappears. "Well," asks Sol, "what are*

---

8. Ibid, p. 56.

9. Ted Cohen, *Jokes: Philosophical Thoughts On Joking Matters* (Chicago: University of Chicago Press, 1999).

10. Ibid, p. 44.

11. Friedrich Nietzsche, *Thus Spoke Zarathustra* in Walter Kaufmann, ed. *The Portable Nietzsche* (New York: Penguin Books, 1976), p. 153.

*they up to? Who are they trying to convert? Why do
they care? Did you get the $1,000?" Indignantly Abe
replies, "Money. That's all you people care about."*[12]

I wouldn't stoop so low as to explain the joke, which I'm sure almost
anyone can get, but I can't help remarking on how brilliantly dialectical is
its underlying philosophy. A Jew, in this comedic (deeply philosophical)
world, is someone who wonders, and who questions. Abe, on entering
the church, gives up this stance of questioning, and succumbs to the
most vulgar materialism. In short, he sells out. But in an absurd reversal,
he projects his own vulgar materialism on Sol, the faithful Jew, the true
questioner. On the surface level, we find laughably ridiculous hypocrisy.
On a deeper level, what is revealed to us is the secret, ironic nature of
ideology, in which truth is not only distorted, but indeed turned into its
precise opposite.

Cohen isn't so convincing when he tries to trace Jewish ironic humor
all the way back to the biblical period. After all, this era preceded
the socially precarious conditions that largely shaped the humor. For
example, he finds evidence of humor in the fact that Abraham and Sarah,
aged one-hundred and ninety, respectively, laughed when informed by
the Supreme Being of their imminent parenthood.[13] Something funny
does seem to be going on, but I suspect that even a couple of dour
centenarian monotheists with an extraordinarily bad sense of humor
might let out some sort of sarcastic laugh at this kind of announcement.

We might imagine Abraham complaining, "I'll be over one-hundred
and twenty by the time I've put him through college, and she (pointing
to Sarah) wants him to go to medical school!" But no such luck in the
original text. Cohen also sees something laughable in the morbid scene
in which Abraham is commanded to stab his son Isaac to death and
then burn him.[14] He's at the point of doing the grisly deed when let off
the hook. The case for divine comedy here might be more convincing
if Yahweh had said something like "Just joking, you schmuck, did you
forget that I'm a benevolent Being!" rather than the grimly serious
"Congratulations, you've just passed the test."

The major problem with Cohen's book is that despite his promise
of "philosophical thoughts," he gives us very little insight into the

---

12 Cohen, p. 41.
13. Ibid, p. 54.
14. Ibid, p. 55.

Détournement by Stephen Duplantier

Certaine gayeté d'esprit conficte en mespris des choses fortuites.
A certain jollity of mind, pickled in the scorn of fortune.
—*François Rabelais*

Anonyme, François Rabelais (1483–1559)
XVIIe siècle, Musée National du Château et des Trianons

Détournement by Stephen Duplantier

L'habit ne fait pas le moine.
A habit does not a monk make.
—*François Rabelais*

Anonyme, François Rabelais (1483–1559)
XVIIe siècle, Musée National du Château et des Trianons

philosophy of humor. This is unfortunate, since he often touches on irony, and irony and philosophy are so intimately interconnected. Take, for example, the famous Zen story recounted by Paul Reps, in which the famous Buddhist philosophical principle of "non-attachment" is illustrated strikingly.

Two monks are walking along a muddy road. They see a beautiful young woman, immobilized at the side of the road, distressed about crossing and ruining her fine dress. One monk quickly picks her up and carries her across. Hours later, after the monks have traveled many miles, the second monk complains, "Why did you pick up that young women? Monks are supposed to avoid contact with women, especially when they're so young and beautiful!" The first monk replies, "What? I put her down hours ago. Are you still carrying her?"[15]

Cohen does veer dangerously in the direction of hard-core philosophy when he observes that a major topic of humor is death. In his opinion, joking about death is a way of "domesticating" it. "It is a way of being in charge, even of death" by "simply being able to speak about it, because if you speak about it, it hasn't numbed you completely, hasn't robbed you of everything."[16]

But this isn't terribly convincing. Though being turned into a complete zombie by something means "not being in charge of it," it does not follow that *not* being turned into a complete zombie by something means "being in charge of it." Death can't be "domesticated," because it goes way beyond the domestic realm. It's about our physical, corporeal, biological, embodied nature—so it challenges all of our socially and egoically bound categories. And this is exactly what links it to the comedic. The Grim Reaper, the ultimate uninvited and unexpected guest, is a natural ironist.

Perhaps ironically, we have to go outside of philosophy to find the best philosophical insights into the comical. Screenwriter and film professor Andrew Horton, author of the book *Laughing Out Loud*,[17] turns out to be much more of a philosopher of humor than either Paulos or Cohen. His topic is writing comedy, but he also delves deeply into the comedic as "a way of looking at the universe."[18] He notes that "comedy" comes from the Greek *komos* (merry-making) and goes back to drunken choruses

---

15. Paul Reps, *Zen Flesh, Zen Bones: A Collection of Zen and Pre-Zen Writings* (New York: Doubleday, 1961), p. 18.
16. Cohen, p. 44
17. Andrew Horton, *Laughing Out Loud: Writing the Comedy-Centered Screenplay* (Berkeley: University of California Press, 2000).
18. Ibid, p. 5.

dressed as animals and shouting insults during Dionysian festivals. In Horton's view, there was from the beginning a link between the comedic and the carnivalesque, both being an expression of "the freedom to turn the world as we know it upside down and inside out without fear of punishment, pain, or consequence."[19]

Horton's view of comedy is very much in the Rabelaisian tradition of carnivalesque humor. As the Russian literary critic Mikhail Bakhtin says in *Rabelais and His World*, the classic work on the subject, carnival celebrates our "temporary liberation from the prevailing truth and from the established order" and proclaims "the suspension of all hierarchical rank, privileges, norms, and prohibitions."[20] It treats all these sacred cows with mocking contempt, and instead affirms through joyful laughter the supremacy of the material and the natural. Carnivalesque laughter is, Bakhtin writes, "the defeat of divine and human power, of authoritarian commandments and prohibitions, of death and punishment after death, hell and all that is more terrifying than the earth itself."[21]

I see this battle between obsessive authority and embodied anarchy each Mardi Gras in the French Quarter of New Orleans, when dismal fundamentalists converge on our hotbed of sin and licentiousness, wielding tracts and placards, threatening revelers with death and damnation. To the great chagrin of these evangelists, the forces of ambiguity and irony—the frenzied dancers and drummers, the feathered and sequined multitudes, the transexual and the transpeciated, the naked and the undead—remain gleefully undeterred.

A problem with aspiring philosophers of humor such as Paulos and Cohen is that they remain too tightly locked into their seriousness to give in to the ribald, anarchic spirit of comedy, especially in its most carnivalesque, celebratory expressions. Cohen is disturbed, for example, by that great ironist Mark Twain's dictum that "against the assault of laughter nothing can stand," replying that "some things should remain standing."[22] And he doesn't mean doing stand-up comedy. Cohen remains too much in the grip of Western rationalism and logocentrism to fully embrace the wildness of the comedic extreme.

However, the mocking, ironic, even outrageous humor of the Trickster and of the Feast of Fools is an indispensible aspect of humor,

---

19. Ibid, p. 7.
20. Mikhail Bakhtin, *Rabelais and His World* (Bloomington, IN: Indiana University Press, 1984), p. 10.
21. Ibid, pp. 90-91. Thus, it is opening oneself to be traumatized by the truly traumatic, the Real itself beneath the mask, the earth.
22. Cohen, p. 70.

From François Desprez's, *Les Songes drolatiques de Pantagruel, ou sont contenues plusieurs figures de l'invention de maistre François Rabelais : & derniere oeuvre d'iceluy, pour la recreation des bons esprits.* Paris : Par Richard Breton, 1565

"...the Fool is often the best of philosophers, the one who turns the most determined philosophers into the worst of fools."

and responds to the deepest levels of our humanity. It is one of the two essential moments of the comedic. Horton identifies these two poles of humor as "the laughter of the ridiculous," in which we "laugh at someone or something," and "the laughter of the ludicrous," in which the laughter "is purely for its own sake."[23]

This recalls a distinction by the Czech writer Milan Kundera, who distinguishes between two kinds of laughter: the "devilish" and the "angelic" varieties.[24] The Devil's laughter expresses a reveling in chaos,

23. Horton, p. 19.
24. Milan Kundera, *The Book of Laughter and Forgetting* (New York: Penguin Books, 1981), p. 62.

an assault on excessive order, authority, and seriousness. The laughter of angels expresses delight in the wondrousness of life and in the mystery of the order and fitness of things. It is an affirmation of being, goodness, and the plenitude of nature, in the face of the destructive forces that would dissolve everything into meaninglessness and randomness. This distinction goes back to ancient times. The Greeks had the mocking, comic god Momus, whose name means "ridicule," but there was also Thalia, the muse of comedy, whose name derives from "blooming," the creative force of nature.

So there is truly a philosophy of humor, and it's a very ancient one. As Wordsworth said of the analytical mind, it often "murders to dissect." And our contemporary philosophers of humor sometimes murder a good joke and kill the spirit of philosophical wonder in their brutally abstract, deadly serious analyses. In reality, the Fool is often the best of philosophers, the one who turns the most determined philosophers into the worst of fools. Yet, despite the efforts of so many philosophers to ruin the joke, philosophy will always be a laughing matter. It reflects the nature of the world that it reflects upon. That world is a generous, gift-giving world. It gives us so much to mock with devilish laughter, and so much to exult in with innocent delight.

Momus Mardi Gras float, New Orleans, 1915

Knights of Momus, The God of Mockery's Parade

Wú

Détournement by Stephen Duplantier

Handa Wanda

Say, Rex is your Ruler Mardi Gras Day
But I'm an ind'an Ruler make kill-a ways
Yeah, an-ind'an roller, y'an-n'an-n'ae
Hey, boy is ya' ready for the Mardi Gras Day?

Don't deny your name
You got your gang
Don't deny your name
You got your fame

You an Indian Ruler, don't give a damn!
(Handa-wanda, Mardi Gras)

Traditional Mardi Gras Indian song

Photography, Surregionalism, and Deep Play

Robert Doisneau photographed the people of Paris as he found them in the streets. His picture of the *flic* striding past the shuttered front entrance of the *Café l'Enfer* in Place Pigalle on the Boulevard Clichy in 1952 is the kind of easy-going, found surrealism many artists have struggled to achieve. By comparison, the self-conscious, overly manipulated surrealist photography of Man Ray seems stilted, removed from real life, and unsure of itself. Doisneau surely felt the natural pulse of the surregional on his walks around Paris.

Left, Hell, 1952, by Robert Doisneau;
right, unknown photographer, Montmartre, Cabarets Artistiques

Originally the giant, fanged demon's mouth had an amanuensis—a smaller demon doorman in a red Satan suit and pitchfork hustling patrons of the red-light district into the baroque cafe interior. The walls of the whimsical café were encrusted with writhing plaster sculptures of grasping demons, and terrifying beasts tormenting the damned (all in all, not too much different from a Catholic Church, minus a high altar, and plus absinthe and champagne). The doorman and the café are long gone, as is the amazing façade itself—probably a victim of the seemingly-perpetual Haussmanization of Paris. This row of artistic cabarets in Montmartre also had a *boîte* named *Le Ciel,* right next door. The theological orientation of the cabaret-goers may have determined which one they entered.

With image manipulation software, unknown to Doisneau who died in 1984, the long-gone infernal façade of the Gate to Hell can be reopened with some digital legerdemain. For the *détournement* of this image in the first chapter of the book, I felt a bit like a photographic felon fooling around with the famous Doisneau image. It was like sneaking into his darkroom and secretly sandwiching some of his negatives together, or bringing some of my own to blend with his, but it's a properly surregional thing to do. I changed the interior of the *Café l'Enfer* to show, not grinning patrons being served beverages by lesser demons, but the neatly-stacked skulls and femurs buried below in the catacombs of Paris—the work of generations of humorously-morbid catalogers of bones.

Doisneau's *flic* seems not to notice the portal to Hell because in the original image, the shutters are drawn. Maybe the cop's daily beat passing the Gargantuan mouth and fangs of Beelzebub had inured him against even the mildest *frisson* of anxiety. After all, here was merely another fallen and harmless Rabelesian giant. Max Cafard has pointed out to me how the giant demon in quiet Clichy reminds him of how in Tibetan cosmology, the terrifying demon is transformed into a protector—a comforting-enough enantiodroma, until one realizes that turning into opposites works in reverse as well and the good can become evil. Maybe the next time the policeman passes the remodeled gate, he'll pause a bit, mentally salute the dead of Paris as he passes the oversized *memento mori* on his walks up the Boulevard de Clichy in Montmartre.

Photojournalist street photographer Robert Doisneau has always been my favorite photographer. He was a paparazzo to the common man. I later found out long after I had admired his work that he was born in Gentilly, just like me, except the faubourg of his birth was in Val-de-Marne, southeast of Paris, and mine was in the Seventh Ward of New Orleans, southeast of Paris Ave. My favorite photograph of his is the picture of children passionately enjoying *Les Guignols Polichinelles* of a street theatre puppet show in Paris. The image shows nothing of the puppets—only the reactions of the children. For me, this was a photography course in one picture, and a clue for where to find the surregional.

Doisneau stalked the people of Paris barely concealed behind his small Leica with a fearless intimacy and an unmatchable aesthetic sense. *His work was nothing if not the deepest play in the city.* Each of his frames was much more than a decisive moment—it was 1/250th of a second of a living tableau, not of a moment, but of whole communities and their intertwined lives seen *tout ensemble*. His photographs now are the record of the life and fabric of a city—a chronicle of his lifelong *dérive*.

Doisneau's daily drifts though Paris photographing the *citadins,* the people of the city, reveal a psychoanthropology as much as a psychogeography of Parisians and their ancient city. Doisneau does so in a generous and reverential way. He chronicled ordinary daily life, but saw the extraordinary in it. He was also part of it all. His daily *dérivisme* was self-referential, but in the same indirect way as the picture of the children laughing at the Punch and Judy show doesn't show the puppets at all. Doisneau photographed himself by photographing the people of Paris. He became—and was—what he beheld.

—Stephen Duplantier

Angela Davis Parkway. Max Cafard and Stephen Duplantier. From monu_MENTAL Group Art Show, Press Street's Antenna Gallery, New Orleans. February, 2012.

Angela Davis Monument on Angela Davis Parkway (formerly Jefferson Davis Parkway in New Orleans). The Angela Davis Monument was created when Angela was named one of the *Ten Most Wanted People to Build Monuments To*. The monument is dedicated to Revolution & Abolition and is located within short marching distance from Orleans Parish Prison, the Center of Incarceration of the USA, the World, and the known Universe.

Afterword

Max Cafard and Stephen Duplantier have been surregional friends and artistic collaborators for decades. They are part of a tribe of surregionalists, artists, writers, musicians, performers, philosophers, poets, geopsychic anarchists, and re-inhabitory ecologists who live in New Orleans and across a wider deltaic disapora.

The surregional space of *L'Isle de la Nouvelle-Orléans* has been tentative land—*la terre tremblante*—for throughout the Holocene era. The land and sea below and around the Isle have created a magical wetland and wet-mind ecology unlike most other places of intertwined natural and human destinies. Surreal by definition, *L'Isle de la Nouvelle-Orléans* spawns expressive cultural forms as different and exotic as the mudlumps of the Mississippi River delta. The delta mudlumps are extrusions of clays and silts caused by the overburden pressure of sedimentation. These small mud volcanoes have cones that spew out flammable gas and mud and can rise abruptly enough to lift a passing ship. The geopsychic analogs to this phenomenon are the cultural mudlumps of *L'Isle de la Nouvelle-Orléans* caused by the overburden pressure of empire and authority. Cultural and artistic mud volcanoes rise abruptly to lift and upend passing ideologies and pomposities.

Surregional inhabitants of *L'Isle de la Nouvelle-Orléans* follow the evolutionary dynamics of island biogeography. The strange hybrid creatures and forms which have evolved and proliferated on the Isle are seen nowhere else. Cafard and Duplantier and their fellow surregionalists explore like Darwin and Wallace, Henry Louis Bates and Alexander von Humboldt, and especially the anarchist geographer Jean-Jacques-Élisée Reclus, finding exotic specimens and marvelling at every oddity and wonder that complex nature and culture throws up. Surregionalism explores and charts the dialectical social ecologies and various *terrae incognitae* of complex, sedimented nature and culture. Cafard, Duplantier and their fellow surregional explorers, the *incroyables,* the *insulaires,* the *habitants de l'isle* in New Orleans, dance and sing the wild *Counja* and discuss with the *Grand Zombí* the song's siren lyric,

> *When freedom comes we shall devour it.*
> *Sweet or spicy, burnt or blazing—*
> *We shall devour freedom when it comes*
> (*Martha Ward's paraphrase of the Counja, or Conjure Song*)

--*Hieronymous Fisch*

Acknowledgments

Thanks to Penelope Rosemont for her encouragement, enthusiasm, and kindness, and for allowing these humble explorations to be associated with her magnificent adventure into surreality. Thanks to Andrei Codrescu, for generosity and inspiration, for opening the Corpse to much of the surregionalist corpus, and for the opening words. Thanks to Steve Duplantier, for exuberant imagination, diligent designing, and a hallucinatory torrent of creative ideas.

Thanks to the many who have given inspiration and support to the surregionalist project in general, or to this work in particular. Among these many are Randall Amster, Aragorn!, Peter Berg (clown patrolling), Jacqueline Bishop, Black Pearl Mutual Aid and Pleasure Club, Eric Bookhardt, Dave Brinks and the Gold Mine of the Imagination, Chris Champagne (yatitude), Rev. Dan and the Church of the Great Green Frog, John Clark (artificial negativity), Crescent City Anti-Authoritarians, Ronald Creagh, Courtney Egan and Press Street, Hieronymous Fisch, Dennis Formento, Jeremias Frogg, Paul Gailiunas and the Troublemakers, Judy Goldhaft, Sandra Guigonis, Jo Guldi, Leenie Halbert and the "Street Named Desire" Communitarian Anarchist Post-K Commune, Helen Hill (Bodhisattvahood), Andy Horton, Eric Jacobson and the Hotel at the Edge of the Abyss, Celina Jeffery and *Drain* magazine, Nathan Jun, Jonathan Katz, Bill Lavender, Peter Marshall, Camille Martin (found message), Tim Morton, NOLA Anarchists, NOLA Free School Network , Gary Oaks (Jesus image), Mary Jane Parker, Danny Postel, Ed Sanders, Kalan Sherard (surregional cartography), Gary Snyder (enduring inspiration), David Watson and The Fifth Estate. Thanks to the Spirits of St. Roch, Place Congo, Jean Lafitte, Marie Laveau, Ludwig von Reizenstein, Elisée Reclus, Joseph Déjacque, and Clarence Laughlin.

Thanks to those who published the texts included in this volume: "Critique of the Dérive" and "Deep Play in the City" originally appeared in *Drain* magazine. "SURREALPOLITIK," "Inter-Galactic Blues," and "The Passion of the Masochrist" appeared in *Exquisite Corpse*. "Giant Economy Size BROTHER" was presented at the International Anarchist Conference on "1984" in Venice. "Laughing Matters" was published by Britannica.com.

Merci à l'Isle de la Nouvelle-Orléans elle-même,
prenant conscience d'elle-même!

Books from Charles H. Kerr

WHAT'S THE USE OF WALKING IF THERE'S A FREIGHT TRAIN GOING YOUR WAY?—Black Hoboes & their Songs by Paul Garon. "A masterpiece of cultural history...Hoboes represented a significant segment of the black working class, and their constant movements were both evidence of constraints and acts of freedom...those who took to the road and their bards have much to teach us about America's 'bottom rail.'" —*Robin D. G. Kelley.* 288 pp., Illus. 25-track CD. paper, $22

DREAMS & EVERYDAY LIFE: André Breton, Surrealism, Rebel Worker, sds, & the seven Cities of Cibola by Penelope Rosemont. "This book is wonderful! I read nothing else till I finished it; a great and passionate evocation of those times–unapologetic and *real.—Diane di Prima* "The personalities, large and small, many of them oddball in the extreme, seemed perfectly suited to a moment in history when, as Rosemont says, life was supercharged with developments that we somehow expected would go on for decades."—*Paul Buhle* 256 pages. Paper $17.

SURREALISM IN '68: Paris, Prague, Chicago. By Don LaCoss. This insightful work of history and analysis brings together the major events of that important year that is so pivital in what came afterward, and gets beneath the surface to the interconnections and the people who were determined to make a difference. 32 pages. $5.

WE WILL RETURN IN THE WHIRLWIND. *By* Muhammad Ahmad. "A major assessment of the 1960s Black radical organizations by one of the major figures involved—a study of the SNCC, the Black Panther Party, the Revolutionary Action Movement (RAM), and the League of Revolutionary Black Workers that only he could have done." —*John Bracey* 350 Pages   Paper $18   Cloth $35

THE BIG RED SONG BOOK: 250-plus IWW SONGS.
Archie Green, David Roediger, Franklin Rosemont, Salvatore
Salerno, *editors.* This book is really a history of the IWW
through its songs. It contains the all-around best collection of
rebel workers' songs and poems ever compiled in English. "A
landscape of hobo-jungles, mountain-mining campfires, ranch
bunkhouses, meetings halls, and free-speech, soap-boxing
rallies marvelously detailed and depicted—*Faron Levesque.*
546 pages. Paper $24.   Cloth $36.

JACQUES VACHÉ and the Roots of Surrealism. By
Franklin Rosemont. "Vaché is magnificent! An important
work!"—*Nancy J. Peters,* "Full of information, subversive
surprises, and wild humor."—*Gale Ahrens.* A bold jaywalker
at the crossroads of history, and an ardent exemplar of freedom
and revolt, Vaché challenged all prevailing values. Conscripted
into the French Army in WWI, where he met André Breton, he
became the major inspirer of the surrealist revolution.
Profusely illustrated 396 pages Paper $20 Cloth $35

HISTORY AGAINST MISERY, by David Roediger. This
collection of 38 articles covers a wide range of topics—football
strikes, the IWW, surrealism, May Day, hiphop, talk-radio, and
writers as varied as André Breton, C.L.R. James, and Sterling
Brown, focused on the oppressive ideologies known as
"miserabilism." "A surrealist roadmap to liberated
futures"—*Robin D.G. Kelley.* 184 pp. Profusely illustrated.
Paper, $18

**THE DEVIL'S SON-IN-LAW: The Story of Peetie Wheat-
straw and His Songs**, by Paul Garon. The classic study of the
influential blues-singer, song-writer, piano- and guitar-
player—one of the greatest and most humorous "characters"
in the history of Black Music. First published in England in
1971, this revised, expanded edition includes a mass of new
information and images, updated bibliography/discography,
and a 24-track CD! 156 pages. $20.

LUCY PARSONS: Freedom, Equality & Solidarity—Writings & Speeches, 1878-1937, edited & introduced by Gale Ahrens, with an Afterword by Roxanne Dunbar-Ortiz. First-ever anthology of the works of Chicago's anarchist and labor agitator. Includes nearly all of her many IWW writings. It adds much to our knowledge of Lucy and her relevance for freedom struggles today. 191 pages. Illus. $17

An Open Entrance to the Shut Palace of WRONG NUMBERS, Franklin Rosemont. Drawings by Cruzeiro Seixas. Exploring the continuities and discontinuities between sleeping and waking, dream and reality, desire and necessity as manifested in misdialed telephone calls, Rosemont finds the Wrong Number to be not only a symptom of alienation and a symbol of the quest for true community, but also a disrupter of reified routine and therefore a *lever* of change. "Strangely endearing and exciting!" —*Oliver Katz.* "A reminder that surrealism is a force that remains afoot in the universe." —*Laura Winton.* 187 pages. Paper $16.

BEN FLETCHER: THE LIFE AND TIMES OF A BLACK WOBBLY. Edited and Introduced by **Peter Cole.** "In a union noted for great organizers, Fletcher (1890-1949) was one of the greatest."—*Carlos Cortez.* 158 pages Paper $18

JOE HILL: The IWW & the Making of a Revolutionary Workingclass Counterculture, by Franklin Rosemont. "The best book ever written on Joe Hill" —*Utah Phillips.* "Direct, passionate, sometimes funny, deeply searching"—*Peter Linebaugh.* "Rosemont seems to have hunted down every available detail of Hill's life and legend; he has spent decades accumulating IWW lore"—*Michael Kazin, L. A. Times Book Review.* 656 pages. Illustrated. Cloth $35. Paper $19.

THE RISE & FALL OF THE DIL PICKLE: Jazz-Age Chicago's Wildest & Most Outrageously Creative Hobohemian Nightspot, edited/introduced by Franklin Rosemont. This Dadaesque open forum was known as "The Indoor Bughouse Square." 186 pages. Paper $14

FROM BUGHOUSE SQUARE TO BEAT GENERATION:
Selected Ravings of Slim Brundage, Founder/Janitor of the
College of Complexes. Edited/Introduced by Franklin
Rosemont. An old Wobbly relates his life in the 1920s
IWW/Bughouse Square counterculture to the Beat Generation
and New Left of the 1950s and 60s. 176 pp. Illustrated. $14.

STORY OF MARY MACLANE & OTHER WRITINGS by
Mary MacLane, edited & introduced by Penelope Rosemont.
This memoir of a rebellious 19-year-old was the publishing
scandal of 1902, praised by writers as different as Clarence
Darrow and Harriet Monroe. MacLane became a frequent
speaker at Chicago's Dil Pickle Club. 218 pages. Illus. $15.

DANCIN' IN THE STREETS! Anarchists, IWWs,
Surrealists, Situationists & Provos in the 1960s. By Franklin
Rosemont & Charles Radcliffe. Critics derided them as "the
left wing of the Beat Generation," but Chicago's *Rebel Worker*
and *Heatwave* (London) were noted for their originality and
uninhibited class-war humor and cartoons. "Thanks for
Dancin'! We surely need it!"—*Diane di Prima.*"Well worth
reading"—*Maximumrocknroll.* 450 pp. Paper $19. Cloth $25

HOBOHEMIA: Emma Goldman, Lucy Parsons, Ben
Reitman & Other Agitators & Outsiders in 1920s Chicago,
by Frank O. Beck. Classic portrait of Chicago's IWW-
influenced counterculture. Illustrated. Cloth $25. Paper $12

CRIME AND CRIMINALS & OTHER WRITINGS by
Clarence Darrow, with essays by Leon Despres and Carol
Heise. The great labor attorney's "Address to the Prisoners in
the Cook County Jail" and other hardhitting indictments of the
U.S. Criminal justice system. 64 pages, Illustrated. $7.50

Please add $2 postage for the first title, and fifty cents
for each additional title.

CHARLES H. KERR PUBLISHING COMPANY
Est. 1886 / **1726 West Jarvis Avenue, Chicago, Illinois 60626**
www.charleshkerr.com   Arcane@ripco.com